Healing
the
Corporate World

How Value-Based Leadership
Transforms Business from the Inside Out

Maria Gamb

NMS Communications LLC

Brooklyn, New York

ISBN 978 0 615 39349-0

Maria Gamb, CEO/CCA
NMS Communications LLC
900 3rd Avenue P.O. Box 320611
Brooklyn, NY 11232
Phone: (800) 527-8186

Praise for Maria Gamb's
Healing the Corporate World

*"**Healing the Corporate World is an inspiring and visionary book** about what it means to change 'business as usual' in the corporate world...Maria Gamb, a successful corporate executive for more than 20 years, writes that **anyone can and should become a change agent.** When we bring our values, such as integrity, collaboration, and esteemable business practices with us to work, this produces greater long-term corporate prosperity and societal good. **This book with its message of hope, is thoughtful, provocative, and is a must read."***
- ERNEST CHU
Bestselling author of *Soul Currency*

*"Maria Gamb shares **a unique and powerful position that every person CAN make a difference, dispelling the notion of helplessness.** She **encourages stakeholders to rise up and be the leader they were meant to be** and walk into the power and influence that can change how business is done. **Powerful. Engaging. Thought-provoking."***
- BRYN Z. JOHNSON
Director, Strategy Consulting, Monster.com
Author of upcoming book *Read the Room*

"Healing the Corporate World opens the door to the new business paradigm that is emerging and so needed today. Illuminating. Enlightening. Practical."
- GREG S. REID
Bestselling author of *Three Feet from Gold*

"Healing the Corporate World is a book for ambitious leaders who are ready to take corporate life to a new level by taking an approach of wholeness to their leadership. Maria Gamb courageously speaks the unspoken truths of corporate life, and simultaneously gives a voice to the unspoken desires and hopes of so many in the business world. In this revolutionary book, she masterfully integrates realities of universal laws into corporate thinking and shows how true value-based leadership comes from the connection to the leader deep within each one of us. Powerful, transformational, and desperately needed in today's corporate world."
- NICOLE HEIMANN
President of 5C! Concept GmbH

"Maria Gamb is a powerful and influential leader who shows others the way to creating success during these radically changing times."
-NEIL WILMOT
Men's Product Development Manager, JAG Australia

"This book goes well beyond discussing "values" as a judgment tool but as each of our motivating and guiding principles in business, life and all our relationships. We are at a pivotal time in business where everything we believed as strong and secure must be re-evaluated. **Gamb provides a step-by-step process to transforming yourself, your business and your bottom line.** *Plus creating a team that wins too! This is* **an invaluable insight into making significant changes across the board!"**
- GLENNA HECHT
Former Director of HR and Current President of Humanistic Consulting

"An excellent book *in restructuring one's thought process on how to be a 'leader of value' today.* **Powerful insights and tools....** *'lead with integrity'. Every individual makes a difference.* **Illuminating! Empowering!"**
- DONNA GIULIANO
Former Vice President, Macy's

"Maria Gamb is a gifted leader and teacher. *She has a unique knack for bridging the gap between universal principles and leadership strategies. She is* **always the voice of reason**...*and what a voice! During these ever changing times, many are desperately seeking ways to take charge of what's going on and make profound, lasting impact.* **There is no one better than Maria to lead the charge for empowered, compassionate and**

*collaborative leadership. The times, they are a changing and **Maria Gamb is beautifully poised as the new voice for the 21st century.***"*
- LIZ PABON
Author of *The MavHERick Mind*

"*Maria Gamb has the guts to take on the very antiquated and outdated systems* that have been pervasive in Corporate America for far too long. *Her very practical and thought-provoking* Seasonal and FARCE systems *should be immediately implemented in every business today. Transformative, Daring, and Powerful. A must-read AND a Must-do!*"
-LAURIE A. SANTOS
Founder of Extreme Dream Training International

*"There seems to be a self-destructive, unspoken code in the corporate world that you should never reveal your pain or fears to others. The **honest and practical models** in Maria Gamb's book Healing the Corporate World can help corporates find **the very things for which they have been secretly wishing, but never had the courage to ask.**"*
- LYNN SERAFINN
Bestselling author of *The Garden of the Soul* and of up-coming book *The 7 Graces of Marketing*

To my parents,
who allowed me to be different.

To my mentors,
who shaped that difference into something
tangible and useful in the world.

I am forever grateful.

Table of Contents

A True Story of Despair and Transformation

I was on a small boat floating in the middle of the Galápagos Archipelago. I'd taken a two-and-a-half-year break from big business to pursue an entrepreneurial endeavor that went south as quickly as it was conceived. That was heart breaking, but the return to office cubicles, fluorescent lighting, and long meetings was an even bigger jolt. So, after an absolutely exhausting fourteen months, I'd fled to the quiet of a sailing trip.

I thought back to how quickly I'd soured on my corporate job after my foray into self-employment. I knew this was not where I wanted to be. It was an extremely toxic environment. Teams were pitted against each other. Screaming matches in the middle of the bullpen, what we affectionately called the giant maze of cubicles where the team resided, were an everyday occurrence. Management had little respect for the employees. Daily, the management team would turn on someone in order to cover up its own failings. Finger pointing was expected. There was no real business plan and no sense of true teamwork. People weren't working together to grow the business. The teams were adversaries, fighting each other for dominance.

A few weeks prior to my leaving for vacation, a peer stormed into my office and began shouting at me. I looked up and told her in a calm voice to "get the hell out of my office and to never speak to me in that tone again." I swiveled around and returned to my work, leaving her screaming in my doorway. Finally, she realized her tantrum had no effect on me and she walked away.

There was no way I was going to entertain her bad behavior. I was too busy recounting the humiliation of sitting in another financial update meeting and seeing that our division was double and triple digits in the red. It was absolutely demoralizing to see the numbers come up on the board. A peer and I sat in the back of the room that morning and slid down in our chairs. Arms folded, hands over our mouths, we were aghast at what we were seeing.

All around me was work that was completely unfocused. The division lacked any real plan or purpose. I had some ideas, but no matter what I said or did, no one seemed to listen. I had spent fourteen years in big business, so I knew we had many problems, but frankly anyone could see why we weren't making any money. In addition to our poor financial performance, the general team was miserable. They were downright fed up, ready to embrace their own inner Norma Rae and go on strike. Admittedly, I was the brainchild behind the idea of storming the elevator banks and taping up signs that detailed the overwhelming general state of anarchy. Had a colleague not talked me out of it, I most likely would have no career left to write about!

But here, off the coast of the Galápagos, everything seemed so peaceful. Life was simple. You got up, put on your wet landing gear and headed for the dingy at the back of the boat. Today we would swim with the sea lions and giant prehistoric turtles. I was looking forward to eight solid days of being completely unplugged—no computers, no email, no text messages or voicemail boxes brimming with nasty messages. On the second-to-last day, we docked at the only inhabited island in the archipelago. I walked around numbly but was grateful to be away from my seasickness medication and the smell of fish. I spotted an Internet café up the street and thought, *Dare I see what's happening in the world today?* I logged in and pulled up my email account. One email demanded to be opened.

"I'm writing you to tell you that I'm leaving the company. I want to thank you for all your support during the time we worked together..." It was a three-page treatise of our history as coworkers, from the woman who had yelled at me constantly, the howler who had stood in my doorway until I swiveled away from the racket. I literally jumped out of my chair and started to dance. Not only had she left, but the residing vice president, whom I considered the fountainhead of poor leadership and captain of a rudderless business, had departed as well. My happy dance continued all the way back to the boat and to New York City a few days later.

Upon entering the company's offices, I knew something was about to occur. I could feel it. Our new vice president, Frank, hovered nearby as I caught up with everyone. His nervous energy surprised me. At last, he called me from his office and asked me to join him and a new member of the management team for a meeting at noon.

Frank has sparkling eyes, a childlike smile, and wire-rim glasses. He's a stocky man—clearly an ex-jock from his youth. But now, his hair was almost fully grey and he seemed quite proud of this sign of aging. Looks are deceiving; this humble man was legendary in the company for his focus and resolve, and for turning businesses around in record time. "Maria, sit down please," he said, and I took a seat, my heart pounding.

"We know that you've been very unhappy with the current state of our business. I respect your opinion. Clearly, having been in this industry for so long, you know there has been a problem here for some time now. So, what I'd like to offer you is a more senior position. I am asking you to make a choice right here and now. Will you be part of the solution or will you continue to be part of the problem here?" He smiled warmly but in his eyes I could see his fierce determination to end the distracting dramas in which our division had engaged. "It's your choice. However, if you choose not to be part of the solution, we'll have to part ways. I only want people who are committed to turning this business around. We'd like you to be our partner in this."

Needless to say, my response was, "Where do I sign?!"

I thought for sure that all the problems would be over. I didn't realize I was standing in the middle of a fierce storm. The realignment would require that we trim some overlapping roles and responsibilities, along with people who would become distraught or frustrated at what they perceived as a loss of power. For the next year, the infighting was intense. Our financial numbers kept slipping. It was painful to watch what seemed like a never-ending spiral downward without feeling hopeless.

I began facing my own demons and questioning my leadership skills. *Am I qualified? Am I strong enough?* I hated having to make some of these tough decisions. I hated that people hated me. I hated me too!

My absolute stubbornness and refusal to quit drove me to work harder than I'd ever worked before. That's really saying something considering I've always been known as someone with a fierce work ethic. But I had worked seventy to eighty hours a week without a day off for more than a year. I worked so much that I really only went home to shower, sleep a few hours and change clothing. It was the most challenging situation I'd experienced in my career. I began to question whether it was my pure stubbornness and tenacity driving me, or I was just completely stupid!

Then, one afternoon, I went shopping with my friend, Nancy, on a rare Sunday when I was not working. My job completely consumed me. As I sipped my tea, tears streamed down my face. "I'm afraid I'm going to land in the hospital, Nance. The stress is that bad."

She looked at me with compassion.

"It seems as if the only way to make all this craziness stop is by literally breaking down. I'm responsible to my team. I can't walk away from this. But I feel my body and my mind breaking down. I don't know how much more I can take."

Nancy urged me to take a vacation, and soon my friends and family, too, began pleading with me to take time off. Realizing they were right—I did need a break—I went to Utah to regain my grounding, joining a group that would be hiking in the mountains. There, the answer to what was going on presented itself to me almost immediately.

After a few nights of sleeping for twelve to sixteen hours, I went on what I would call a "meditation hike" in order to regain my sense of self. The guide for my group took us to a secluded portion of the canyon and instructed us to begin ascending a beautiful, little white-capped mountain set high above all the other red rock formations around us. He said, "Walk silently, and when the time feels right, find a spot and sit down. Then, ask the universe whatever question you need answered and silently await the response."

From the mountain's peak, I peered out at my natural surroundings, which were truly gorgeous. I sat there, quietly, trying to figure out what to do, to ask, to say. Finally, words came to my mind: *Why does this keep happening to me? It's the same pattern over and over again. Why am I tirelessly giving to the brink of exhaustion? I seem to always get to this point with any job, but this time it's worse!*

I waited, silently, and then my answer came. This is what Spirit told me:

Who are you?
You are spirit and light.
When you honor and respect yourself, you honor and respect me.

I started sobbing. I realized I hadn't respected the divinity in myself. All this craziness around me was self-created. My situation was just what I "expected" it to be. It was familiar to me. I had embraced principles that were now playing out in my life, and I couldn't blame anyone else for the results I was reaping.

I decided at that moment I would have to figure out just how I was contributing to my suffering—pronto! So I said, "Okay, I'm done with this I'm ready to stop this crazy cycle. I don't know how to change. Show me! Just show me." I sat with this intention in my heart until I felt it was time to go back down the mountain.

Shortly after returning from my hike, I met a lovely woman at the resort, who listened to my story of receiving this profound insight. She suggested that my own limiting beliefs were playing out in my life. The minute she said that, my mother's words ("What you say is what you'll get!") came flooding back into my mind. I thought about what my mother had taught me about cause and effect, and attracting situations that matched my inner state of being. As a teenager, I'd been exposed to what I was now realizing were universal truths. How could I have forgotten this powerful wisdom?

I thought back to a game my mother and I would play together. We'd purposely set out to create or manifest situations or things, and be delighted when we succeeded in attracting and creating what we desired. I was accepted into the college of my choice and got into the internship program I so desperately wanted. I visualized the apartment I wanted to buy and the salary I wanted to be paid. All of it came to me exactly as I'd imagined it. It was as if I'd hidden these tools away in my sock drawer for the past dozen or so years!

Making the Connection

Everything that's going on around you is a direct reflection of what's going on inside you. Your thoughts create your circumstances. What's happening in your life is a direct reflection of who you believe you are, and what you think you must endure in order to achieve your goals. If what is inside you is being reflected outside of you, it's your responsibility to change internally so you'll bring about different external results. Your environment will mirror your true interior state of belief. That day in Utah, I realized my inner worth was crystallizing all around me. That worth wasn't so worthwhile.

Waking up to the very harsh reality that my difficulties at work were of my own making was like getting a metaphysical smack between the eyes. And it was exactly what I needed.

I realized that every single fear and worry about my abilities manifested situations that matched up with my anxiety. The staff mutiny that had gone down several weeks before was a reflection of my own insecurities. My tremendous frustration that nothing was changing was a result of my own lack of belief it actually would. The insanely long hours I put in and my intense pace were indicative of what I thought I had to do in order to achieve success. I was constantly pushing, pushing, and pushing some more. Hello, can you say, "control freak"? Did I have trust issues! Most of the time it felt like my team was forcing a twenty-pound watermelon through a tea strainer. It was *not* pleasant.

But in this very moment of realization, I knew the circumstances at work wouldn't change until there was a change in myself. Only then would my team and our results shift.

I also realized my beliefs mirrored the beliefs of the leaders above me in the office hierarchy. We were all tied into this strange, little drama, causing us to compromise ourselves in order to achieve success. Because of the "bottom-line" and "profits-at-any-cost" mentality driving business, people perceive that if there are no immediate results, there's no success. Up until this point, people had been steeped in fear and were engaging in egocentric decision-making as they stepped on hands and heads to reach the top. Now, however, I had a chance to shift this in my own work life. Things could be different, but first, *I* had to be different.

When I thought back to my long career, I realized this fear-based, egocentric way of doing business was a pattern that had presented itself time and time again in my own attitudes and behaviors, as well as those of the people I'd worked with. In fact, I was one of the lucky ones. I never had staplers or chairs thrown at my head—yes, some of my friends and colleagues had experienced that. I've never been in an organization where the leadership compromised the employees' retirement plans for the sake of their own greed. No leader in any organization I've worked within was led away in handcuffs from the offices. In fact, I had a pretty good set of mentors along the way.

However, competitiveness, a lack of integrity, isolationism, a scarcity mindset, and "giving in order to get" are rampant today. An organization's problems may not be splattered across *The New York Times* or the evening news, but they will be reflected in how individuals in the company interact with each other on an everyday level.

The team members may share good values at the core, but if people are only concerned with their own self-esteem and need for recognition and love, they will behave in ways outside of their true nature. This happens quite often. When someone says, "I behave with great integrity and it is part of my value system" then undercuts a colleague in order to get ahead, their underlying, subconscious motivation has taken over.

Too often, people in organizations operate not from their core values but from the fear that they won't get their needs met. Consequently, they generate results that reflect this fear and self-centeredness. They create an atmosphere of competitiveness and adopt a "me first" attitude.

Many leaders in business have wondered if theirs is the only organization that works this way. Given the number of businesses collapsing and slashing staff these days, clearly that's not the case. Values based in fear, lack, and competitiveness have brought about problems that have now bubbled up to the surface. These values simply no longer contribute to the bottom line in a healthy way.

According to the Bureau of Labor Statistics, the unemployment rate rose from around 4 percent in 2007 to 7.6 percent in January of 2009.[1] Congress began to bail out banks and financial institutions at the end of the Bush administration in 2008, and continued to do so into the new Obama presidency. The failures of so many seemingly strong, large corporations shocked many.

Now, the values of business, the very way corporations operate, is in question—especially when one big bank that received a bailout went on to spend hundreds of thousands of dollars on a spa vacation for their management and top earners. Some Wall Street executives continued to collect their multimillion-dollar bonuses even as workers in many different industries lost their jobs. In many companies, the disease of fear and greed that leads to unsustainable practices is no longer contained within the walls. It is now out there for the world to see.

The healing of the corporate world must start on the inside. The very way we think, behave, and interact in business must change. If you're a leader of an organization struggling to make sense of unprecedented changes in the economy and keep your team motivated and successful, or a senior manager who feels caught in the crossfire between the ultimate head honcho and the workers who make the business happen, this book offers you tangible, real solutions. It helps you become the catalyst for change. The simplicity of the cure to the disease affecting business today may surprise you.

So what is the prescription for healing?

- **Recognize your power.** Healing begins with *you*.

- **See the big picture.** The world is reflecting what's going on inside of you and others.

- **Be open to change.** You must align your beliefs with your core values and let go of a scarcity mindset.

- **Understand how the universal laws apply to business.** By working with these laws, you can make the internal changes that lead to new, better results.

- **Choose your higher self over your ego self.** Know when you're operating from the fearful ego self and aim instead to work from your higher self, which is free of fear and the perception of scarcity.

- **Act from your higher self.** Correct your course and realign with your core values whenever you find yourself drifting back into the old way of operating.

- **Give the best you've got.** Give, and you'll bring about the results you desire without having to be a "go getter."

- **Be a change agent.** Start to make a value stand and take a definitive action.

- **Choose your team.** Your team's values need to reflect and complement yours. Is your team ready to embrace a new, healthier set of values?

- **Collapse competitiveness.** Collaboration will strengthen your team and your organization.

- **Foster creativity and innovation.** To make your business sustainable and promote growth, you have to allow creativity to flourish.

All of this may seem radical, but the current business climate shows it's time to stop clinging to the old ways and find the courage to make big changes. The transformation begins with you. You can no longer wait for someone else to lead the way.

It's up to you to begin the process *now*.

The Starting Point for Healing Is *You*

"**I** can't make a difference here! There are too many obstacles and the bureaucracy is ridiculous." A colleague sat in my office feeling utterly defeated. Shaking his head and looking at his shoes, he insisted, "This is an impossible task. Who am I to think I could fix this company's problems? I have no real clout here!" Although he was a senior manager, he still felt he had no real chance at success. "There's no way one person could make any significant changes in a business so large it resembles a giant cruise ship!" At one time or another, this sort of fear and doubt besets all of us.

The healing of the corporate entity has to start with the individual. It doesn't even matter at what level you participate. Whether you're part of an organization and you manage others, or you're simply an employee, you can be part of the solution. However, it's the role of leaders to take charge and blaze a new path. The key to returning any ailing business to functionality and profitability lies within the people in that organization and their mindsets. People may be any company's greatest asset, but their consciousness and awareness is the raw material that holds the greatest potential for change.

Strong business plans and robust spreadsheets with positive projections are valuable. In fact, having a clear vision and plan is critical to a company's success. But unless the leaders get their heads and hearts straight, changing their thoughts, beliefs, and actions, they will only see more of the same kinds of results. It's time to redefine the role of business in society, so people become more connected to the solution. It's time to realign the way we operate in business. The bottom-line and financial success is important for our economy, but it's now time for business to play a new, more positive role in society as well.

It may be hard to believe you can truly make a difference in your company and help them switch out of the old, unproductive mindset. There may be many layers and levels of workers and managers above and below you. No one will do everything perfectly, no matter how excellent your plan for change. You will not win every battle. During the process of transformation you may not always behave as you would like. As you begin to deploy a different kind of leadership, the changes may be so subtle you don't even notice them at first. However, as every little change occurs it builds upon the preceding ones, until all the changes make a big and evident difference.

Many of these ideas may not be new to you. You may think, *Of course, that makes complete sense*, yet others in your company may look at the changes you're making and think you've lost your mind. Most will probably not care one bit that you're working with universal laws and principles (as you'll learn more about in Chapter 5). They'll be more concerned with the results, and how it feels when they come into the office each day.

The beauty of this process of becoming a change agent and participating in healing a business is that it demonstrates what happens when people tap into what's already inside them, and take action instinctively—a true reflection of divine inspiration as well as natural intuition. The changes may be awkward at first, but once the grip of fear is loosened, the business will begin to operate differently. There is a sense of security that comes when you allow the life jacket you're wearing to support you and help you float. As you trust in your new, sustainable way of operating, every part of you relaxes and you begin to enjoy the experience. Struggle and strain cease.

The guiding principles you'll learn about in this book are powerful. I have seen these principles return a division to profits and become an organization's benchmarks for success. I've had the pleasure of being a part of teams determined to generate profits without sacrificing integrity. Our results weren't perfect, nor were any of us for that matter. Now, looking back, I am amazed at the divine beauty of the experiences I've had helping companies to align with these principles. Steve Jobs said in a commencement speech at Stanford University several years ago, "You can't connect the dots looking forward: you can only connect the dots looking backwards."

In this book, I am connecting the dots from my many years of experience in big business. There is a way of doing business in the real world that mirrors the way the spiritual and metaphysical realms operate, and which creates success. All it takes is one person to begin the process of transformation. That person is you.

For the process to work, you must be willing to accept personal responsibility for transforming. Once you do, you can begin the shift within yourself first, and then begin to influence those around you. To make this transformation, you'll need to examine and correct the value and beliefs systems on which you operate. These two steps will help you understand that you're standing on the verge of a profound new beginning, and that you have the power to alter the course of your business. Rather than look at the hopelessness around you and give in to fear and cynicism, I invite you to see the enormous opportunity you have to create a new beginning.

Make no mistake, this is a huge paradigm shift. As a leader, you have immense power to transform your team, your organization, and your company's bottom line by shifting your own internal climate. This singular shift within—that of your own mindset—can result in remarkable transformations in the workplace, as well as in your personal life.

Buckle Up, It's Going to Be a Bumpy Ride

I'm going to be completely honest with you: At first, shifting the way you operate in business is not going to be easy. People will resist your changes, push back, and be outright mean to you. They'll react badly because you'll be threatening their internal programming, which is as old as they are. Most people have been conditioned to have a particular mindset about business and to act in accordance with beliefs such as:

- "Winner takes all!"
- "Defeat is for the weak!"
- "Survival of the fittest!"
- "Win at any cost!"

Though we've been playing by the rules of this mindset, we're now unhappy with the results we've been getting. In many respects, this mindset is too rigid and restrictive.

A business is much like a body. Every business enterprise needs a spine. It needs a framework that can hold it and sustain it, which allows information to move through the body with ease. It also needs flexibility in this spine that enables it to adapt to the conditions around the body.

Our old thought system exists at one extreme on a spectrum of control. It could be classified as a framework with many rules, a great deal of rigidity, hierarchy, and excessive control. In this scenario, it's as if a metal rod allowing little to no flexibility is confining the spine of our enterprises. This is very much the state we've been operating within that has been founded on distorted values of achieving and success.

In a restrictive, highly punitive structure, team members spend more time looking to find blame and inflict judgment on one another than on fixing problems or stepping up to the plate and saying, "I made a mistake. This is what happened. Now let's fix it." We need to move away from this model because it is stifling growth and progress.

I am not, however, advocating that we throw the baby out with the bathwater. Oftentimes, as human beings we think the solution is to go to the polar opposite of what we're seeing. In this instance, that would mean going to the extreme of having fewer rules, and more freedom and permissiveness to express one's self outside of any kind of boundaries. The New Age thought process "It's all good," where no one is confined to any rules or code of conduct is an example of this extreme. A business that uses this type of thought system values the validation of others more than it values the mission of the group.

If this mindset were a body, it would have no spine or structure. But without taking some kind of form, the business entity cannot function properly. In organizations where there is no formal structure, accountability, and flow of information, nothing happens. Decisions are not made and all good ideas stay in the dream state, never being fully realized. As in the rigid thought system, highly permissive business structures stifle growth and progress. They allow people to use their wounds to escape taking personal responsibility. We need to find a balance between these two polarities.

Although these two mindsets are on opposite extremes of a spectrum, there is a commonality between them. The first group, the rigid group, is trying to gain love, acceptance, and recognition by achieving at any cost. The second group, the too-flexible group, is trying to gain love, acceptance, and recognition by wallowing in their emotions.

The first group is all about doing and taking action. The second group is all about dreaming, with very little action being taken. What we are talking about in this chapter is finding the middle ground. We're looking to create a business paradigm that includes creativity, flexibility, planning products and services, and execution plans, all while treating others with dignity and respect. This chapter is about establishing a natural flow that is constantly circulating between all these modes.

When the rigid thought process is dominant, we end up with a system that is too focused on survival and short-term profits. It is not sustainable. This distorted system has rules that are based in ego: greed, selfishness, fear, and narcissism. The focus is not on the long-term growth of the business or its people.

In spiritual terms, the opposite of the ego and fear is the higher self and love. The higher self is not greedy, selfish, fearful, or narcissistic; it's the exact opposite. It is the part of us that's been forgotten and neglected—and it's the key to unlocking the healing of organizations and the teams that reside within them. It's also the key to bringing back the creative force, which leads to innovation, resilience, new products and services being developed, and innovative marketing. It allows a company to flourish in the long-term.

To access creativity, you have to change your mindset and embrace the balanced approach, which includes how you interact with your staff and vendor base.

Realize that what you're about to do is break a paradigm that has been in place for a very long time. We have become accustomed to the fear-based, competitive, ego-driven culture of big business. However, now it's time to make a choice. Do you want to continue on the same course, which has landed business in general in a heap of trouble, or do you want to move forward? Do you want to travel the road that has led to breakdowns, or the road that leads to breakthroughs? You're at a crossroads.

Choose.

If you're reading this book, you're one of those leaders, like myself, who sincerely wants to help your company and support those in positions above you, but also the teams that toil so hard and have seen very little success and reward. You may feel this is your last chance, and that you're at a breaking point. But even if you're deeply frustrated and thinking about giving up, you may realize that something inside of you longs to understand why you are here in this company, at this time, and what your role is. Perhaps you see the suffering of others around you and you desperately want to help. Maybe you say you're willing to do whatever it takes to stop the downward spiral because you have to—your heart, soul, and spirit will not allow you to walk away. Not yet.

Welcome to the role of change agent.

You are going to take the road to breakthroughs. It is a spiritual journey and a return to your true self.

Chapter 2

See the Bigger Picture

W hen you look at what's going on today in the business world, you have to wonder what the leaders of so many of these floundering megalithic companies were thinking.

An Important Reflection Period

The economic crisis that revealed itself in September 2008 was sobering for people in big business. Even if you weren't part of that community, the effects of prestigious establishments failing so dramatically rippled into all corners of the economy. Mismanagement of funds, false reporting of homeowners' earnings, predatory lending, overly complex financial products that spread the damage of toxic mortgages, undercapitalization, and many other demonstrations of greed, ego, and a problematic value system were splashed across the newspapers daily. It was nearly impossible to believe anyone could escape the deluge of negativity. Every news program, blog, and newspaper was filled with doom and gloom reports about the state of the economy.

What happened on Wall Street and among mortgage lenders, banks, financial institutions, insurance giants, and investors couldn't have happened if it weren't for the leaders in these fields having an ego and fear-based mindset that governed their actions and produced devastating results. And when I say "leaders," I not only mean the top dogs on the chow line, but also people in all levels of management: senior, middle, and departmental. The number of people collaborating on schemes that temporarily created the illusion of wealth, only to cause economic disaster later on, was huge.

You could tell me you are powerless and therefore not responsible. But I assure you it doesn't matter what anyone above you on the corporate ladder says. You could be in disagreement with their values and their ideas about the way the company should operate. You could say that if you speak about making changes, no one will listen to you. I understand. I have felt that way, too. You might say, "But, Maria, you don't know my business or where I work."

That may be true, but whatever your situation, however difficult it is to bring everyone together in agreement on your company's values and plans, here's the bottom line: You can feel like a powerless victim for as long as you like. You can continue to allow others to decide your fate, your future, and your economic status and stick with the status quo, because you're afraid of what will happen if you make any moves. Or, you can be brave enough to go within and begin to make the changes you need to make inside yourself, to begin the process of healing *where* you work by changing *how* you work.

The change you want to see must start with you, the individual. What's going on inside you will be directly reflected back to you by your team and everyone else around you, from your customers to your support staff.

Are you skeptical that you can make profound changes within your company? My question is, do you really have a choice to stick with the old way of operating? Consider this: The current business model isn't working anymore. The "dog-eat-dog," "win at all costs" mentality has led to undeniable disaster. Perhaps you don't care about "universal truths" or achieving a "spiritual" mindset. Nonetheless, something has to change.

Sadly, sometimes the only way to get some people's attention is to hit them in the pocket. Guess what? Profits aren't what they used to be. Someone has already come in and lifted your wallet from your pants or purse. The power of your bankcard and credit cards, and your financial security are gone. You're looking over your shoulder wondering whether you could lose your job in the next round of cuts. You've been hit where you live.

It's time to make a choice.

Divine Chaos

"Divine chaos" is the best term to explain the current state of affairs. Chaos may sound like a bad thing, but it is not. You must understand that although chaos may be destructive, it is also a course corrector. *Chaos is the literal and figurative dismantling of a system and its beliefs*. Chaos occurs when systems and beliefs are out of alignment with the core values of any group. Universal laws govern us all. Our current economic chaos is a sign that our value system and our beliefs about commerce are out of sync with these spiritual truths. The only way through the chaos is to wake up, remember our authentic selves, and act with truth, integrity, and transparency. When we accept and work with the universal laws this will improve our ability to bring about the results we desire.

Old beliefs and ways of operating are giving way to a new structure based on higher consciousness. Making surface changes won't be good enough. Applying a Band-Aid won't work in our current situation. There *must* be a dismantling of what is not working, in order for new growth to occur and restore us to health.

Several years ago, I was living in Melbourne, Australia. The Blue Mountains in New South Wales were up in smoke—not with little fires, but with major fires that engulfed the area and left a wide swath of destruction. One day over lunch I expressed my dismay at the situation to a dear friend of mine. "It's terrible. People are losing their homes and this beautiful region is being devastated."

My friend looked at me with a very strange expression and said, "And why does this surprise you? It's the natural course of nature. For that region to regenerate itself, there must be a fire. The underbrush has to be burned away and the heat has to be generated if many of the plants indigenous to this region are to reproduce. You see, the seedpods can't open without heat. This is the way nature renews itself. People who live here know this. They know the risk of building their homes in an area where wildfires appear, and they take it on willingly. They accept that this is the course of nature. If something new and more magnificent is going to appear, that old underbrush must be released."

This story illustrates nature in action. The natural order is that life always regenerates itself. Chaos may ensue in order to facilitate this process. It may not always be in the same exact form, but life will and does regenerate. One thing passes away and dies, and new life always replaces it. It is a never-ending cycle.

Nature as It Relates to Business

The current chaos in the corporate world is much like the wildfires I saw burning in Australia. We can expect something new to emerge from the chaos. The old business model rooted in fear no longer works. It has wreaked havoc on people's finances and shaken them to the core. A shift is necessary and, in fact, inevitable. People are demanding and creating it. Certain ways of operating will be discarded as we go forward.

Complacency formerly blinded us, but now we are waking up to the illusions we embraced. The smoke is in the air and we're still standing and watching it with shock and confusion. The seriousness of the situation has come to light; we can no longer ignore it.

At this time, we need to completely reevaluate the way we've been operating. For this to occur, the old business model had to collapse. You can't build something new on a foundation that is broken, fragmented, or cracked. It's just never going to work. Consider this period of chaos the "burning off" period, nature's way of saying, "I'm getting rid of all this junk so you can start again. You can create something new. Different. Stronger."

To clear out the damaged foundation in your business, you must explore your beliefs and motivations for leading and behaving the way you have been. Clearing out the old, dead way of operating is an important element in the process of making way for new meaning, new ideas, and new prosperity. If you continue to rely on the same old business model and belief system associated with it, the results you achieve will never be any different from what they are today. By doing the same thing over and over again, you will keep getting the same results.

The reality is that business is just like nature. At the core of regeneration and renewal of life are ideas, innovation, and divine, creative inspiration, all of which create a tangible product. The creation of jobs and opportunities in the marketplace and revenue perpetuate life, resulting in sustainable businesses and a sustainable economy. In nature, everything changes and cycles.

When a business becomes stagnant, its ideals and belief systems outdated, its creativity dried up, it stops regenerating. Without new ideas it will enter an autumnal phase of life and die. Unless its leaders can then drop their competitiveness, discover what is valuable to them, and establish a new flow of innovation, opportunity, money, and other resources in their organization, there can be no hope.

Realize that the Cycle is Inevitable

The way the leaders of an organization behave will determine the pace of the growth for any business. It could be growing, as it would be in springtime, or dying, as it would be in the autumn. How many times have you been in an environment where any or all of the elements crucial for growth—ideas, innovations, opportunities, money, resources—were suppressed? Why do you think that was so? Fear? Insecurity? Control issues? All are good answers. Asking the questions, "How has growth been stifled?" and "How have I contributed to this?" is an important start in clearing out the old to make way for the new. Remember, the responsibility for change starts with you first. We no longer have the time or perceived luxury of blaming others.

I'd like you to consider nature's seasonal cycles. We all experience them to some degree, no matter where we live. While some regions may see snowstorms in the winter, others may experience heavy rains or some other manifestation of nature's cleansing process. Then, a few months later, those same regions see the budding of leaves, the flowering of fruit trees—springtime—and later in the year—in summer—a harvest.

Within each season of the natural cycle in business, specific questions are being asked of us on both a personal and professional level. Each season reflects an opportunity to shift awareness to prepare for the next step in our personal cleansing or regeneration, which is then reflected in our business interactions. Each season also contains a gift and a risk. The lack of courage and conviction could cause us to become stuck in a particular season.

We'll begin by looking at the autumn of the business cycle, since business in America is in this period. Inevitably, we shall pass through to other seasons. Ideally, we would lead ourselves through the seasons on purpose because we know it is most efficient.

Autumn

Autumn is a natural part of the business cycle in any company. This is a time in which we see what the seeds we planted long ago produced. It is a time to take stock of what has been harvested and to let go of what doesn't work. As we look back today, it is obvious that some wonderful opportunities appeared in the past two decades. There have also been some very obvious shortfalls in the business landscape. In autumn, our task is to objectively look at everything that has happened and learn from our mistakes.

Recently, we have realized something has gone horribly wrong on our watch that needs to be remedied. Until now, we were unaware of the negative consequences of our choices—or perhaps we recognized them but were too timid or afraid to go against the majority and say something. Now, we have no choice but to do the work of autumn.

Autumn is the time of *The Reveal,* a moment when individuals look around and ask themselves, *What the heck just happened?* Sometimes this is going to feel as if we've been in a car traveling at high speed without a seatbelt, and we've hit a wall. How did what seemed to be working so well go sour so quickly? This often happens even in our personal relationships. However, not all autumnal stages need to come as a result of a disastrous situation. Sometimes it is going to feel fun and easy. For example, autumn is a natural stage after finishing a project or the end of a process where you want to assess what worked and what didn't. Ideally, you want to build autumn into your regular process, so you can be proactive rather than reactive to what is going on around you.

During *The Reveal,* fear and anger can emerge. We may see ourselves as victims, and feel that our trust has been betrayed. We may want to run and hide rather than face the truth of all that has occurred. Our confidence may have been shaken by events.

Each person senses that he bears some responsibility for the results (good or bad) and begins to question his part in the scenario, asking, "Did I compromise myself in any way? Was I an effective contributor? Did I enable (to any degree) a downturn to occur by playing follow the leader, when I knew it was immoral and unethical to do so? Did my actions (to any degree) produce these results? Where have I placed my trust? What or who gives me a sense of security?"

These types of questions and observations are the part of *The Reveal* where the gift of the season is discovered. The gift is letting go of that which no longer works. We not only see the problems, missteps, and the ego distortions that have occurred and led our organization to become less profitable and effective, we begin to understand why they happened. By recognizing and understanding what went wrong, we can now discard ways of operating and values that are no longer viable.

The risk during this period is to fall into feelings of guilt, hopelessness, and resignation, believing that the past dictates the future; that you've failed and will continue to do so. Guilt is a paralyzing factor. When the flaws in the system have been revealed, we feel insecure and afraid to make another mistake. Our guilt only compounds this insecurity, making us fearful all over again. It's a vicious cycle.

However, as we let go of flawed processes we develop hope. Hope is the antidote to guilt and resignation because it offers us the opportunity to feel enthusiastic, excited, and optimistic about the possibility that something better lies beyond what we may be experiencing in the present. It offers us the chance to become aware of where we can make corrections and improvements. Hope erases guilt because it allows us to view the past without becoming paralyzed by it. It allows us to learn from our experiences and find the courage to move forward into something new.

To transition from fall into winter you must first have some level of understanding of the cause of your results. We will discuss cause and effect in great depth in Chapter 4. You cannot correct or improve upon something you don't comprehend. Embracing hope is the catalyst that allows you to pass into the next season, which is winter.

Autumnal Summary: *The Reveal*

Gift / Lesson:
- Letting go of what no longer serves you

Risk:
- Guilt, resignation and/or hopelessness

Antidote:
- Hope

Winter

The natural progression of the business cycle is to move from autumn into winter. Winter is a time of deep reflection and introspection, a period known as *The Evaluation.*

Winter is a gestation period in which we begin to imagine a return to core values, such as honesty, trust, transparency, respect, and vulnerability. We evaluate what we care about and want to bring forward, and determine which of our business practices and behaviors we wish to retain. The very foundations of who we are being are reevaluated—and may even be replaced—as we decide what components (including how we will wield our power and influence) will make up a new foundation going forward.

We begin to question the basis of our security and worth, asking, *"What is it that is truly important?"* and *"How can I become a vital part of this organization's future, helping it to survive and evolve?"* We assemble building blocks for a new beginning, as we evaluate our values and whether we're remaining true to them.

The gift of winter is reclaiming our identity, including our spirituality. As we engage in evaluation, we typically get in touch with our spirituality and inner source of guidance, which gives us an opportunity to redefine our role as a business leader. During the winter phase of the business cycle we are in an excellent position to remember that we aren't simply leaders — we're spiritual beings having human experiences, and that we're here to serve. Recognizing our true nature lets us reconnect with the highest good and discover our greatest potential. If we do so, we can reclaim our personal power and release any harsh feelings. Then we can move forward and do what we need to do.

The risk of winter is falling into self-absorption and narcissistic obsessing over everything we did or did not do in the past. Evaluation is important, but excessive doubts about our abilities can cause us to spiral into a cycle of shame, where we become overly self-critical and unable to move forward. Shame, negative self-judgment, and self-doubt cause us to procrastinate, sabotage our efforts to change, and even become passive-aggressive.

The catalyst to move forward out of winter is finding the courage to take action. Without taking action there really is no animation to courage. That is why it is so important to be very clear when you realize it will take courage for you to move forward — the momentum to, indeed, move is taking a specific action.

Winter Summary: *The Evaluation*

Gift / Lesson:
- Reclaiming your identity and determining what's truly important

Risk:
- Narcissistic tendencies, self-absorption, cycle of shame, self-criticism

Antidote:
- Courage coupled with action

To reach a new beginning and plant the seeds of greater outcomes, we need to make a *value stand*. Up to the moment of the value stand, all the work leaders do is internal. At this critical turning point between the old and the new, between winter and spring, the leader's work moves into the external environment, where his values become visible by his actions.

Making a Value Stand

Before we can create a new beginning in spring we are at a *Course Correction Transition Point,* standing between the old paradigm and the unknown new world that lies ahead. As painful as the prior periods may have been, we recognize that without them, we would not change the way we conduct business. We wouldn't be forced to look at our role in the pruning away of our previous habits, which no longer serve an organization or us. The debris on the forest floor, left over from the old ways, needs to be burned off before any new growth can emerge.

Autumn and winter collectively give us an opportunity to assess, evaluate, and reflect upon the past and learn from it. We are asked to redefine ourselves, reconnect with our spiritual selves, reclaim our core values, and make a value stand to show how we will operate in the future. During this period, when we make a value stand, we are asked to take positions on loyalty, betrayal, forgiveness, and generosity to those around us, to decide how much we value these qualities and actions.

We are asked to release our resentments and let go of hidden agendas, false posturing, secrecy, and competitiveness. We're called to return to a natural state of balance by removing all our defensiveness, offensiveness, and need to justify our actions. The ego's excesses, which have caused many of the problems of the past, need to be discarded so we can focus on answering the important question *"What do I need to do now to make a change? And how?"*

What can get in the way of moving forward (the root of our fear) is pride. We don't want to look foolish by making a mistake, so we remain isolated, afraid to trust others, and even adopt a martyr complex. Unfortunately, until we make a value stand and demonstrate with our actions what we've learned in fall and winter, we haven't integrated our lessons. We only have an intellectual understanding of what our shift will be like and not embodied comprehension.

The prideful person is resistant to change and working with others. He arrogantly defends his refusal to budge by insisting he knows everything, he's heard it before, there's nothing for him to learn, and no one has anything of value to tell him. With blinders firmly in place, he finds it extremely difficult to admit he's made any mistakes. If he does, he downplays them and insists only he can make the minor changes or adjustments needed to make the business run beautifully again.

The need to maintain control and adherence to the illusion of perfectionism are problems rooted in insecurity and fear. These feelings cause people to isolate themselves, which, in business, often results in them being left behind by their teams. That's why taking the action is the catalyst essential for ending winter. You must act according to values that may or may not be openly shared by your colleagues and competitors.

One other important factor in this portion of the cycle is to understand that redefining your key, core value positions is not a license to judge others for their choices. It is not a measuring stick or a means to make yourself "right" and others "wrong" for their beliefs. It is, however, the measure for your life, how you decide to live, interact, and engage others. We are talking about you and your personal responsibility.

A simple equation can be used to further illustrate how to define this concept:

Core Value + Value in Action = a specific result

1) Identify your core value (the noun) – honesty, integrity, transparency etc. This is also termed the **competency value** you wish expressed.

2) Identify the value (the verb) – how will the competency be demonstrated as an accountability, or the **means value.**

Using the core value of honesty you can structure this belief into quantifiable terms with this formula, rather than just merely words without action or guidelines.

Example #1:
I will be honest in my dealings with my staff, suppliers, and the people I market and sell to by never deploying scare tactics to get my way.

Example #2:
We conduct business in an honest manner, holding each individual staff member, supplier, and client in the highest regard, treating each with the utmost respect.

Example #3:
We promise to always be straightforward, honest, and direct. No bull, no hype, no canned slogans or misleading advertising campaigns.

This is your value stand. They are the terms of engagement for yourself and your staff. You can have one or two. You can have four or five. Whatever you wish. Communicate them in whatever terms you care to: formally or informally. However, being clear is essential for all involved to embrace its meaning and intention. These are part of a new foundation upon which you will build your business relationships.

Value Stand Summary:
Course Correction Transition Point

Gift / Lesson:
- Define key core value positions

Risk:
- Pride and judgment of others

Antidote:
- Willingness to change

Once the value stand(s) have been identified and quantified, you move forward into spring. Without making this adjustment you will repeat the same old patterns, mistakes, and results of the past.

Spring

Spring is a time for planting new seeds and watching the seedlings begin to push through the soil and into the light of day. It is the season of *The New Beginning*. It's as if all the old has been cleared away and there is a fresh patch of ground waiting for imagination to come forth and bloom.

Spring is a crucial time in the business cycle because without new growth in industry, business has no real viability. Without the opportunity to create a fresh start, free from the problems of the past, we could not create new opportunities and new positions to be filled.

Every new beginning takes place on several planes at once: the spiritual plane, the psychological plane, and the physical plane. In the business world, the physical plane is the tangible form of commerce, which is the most basic function of business. In addition to creating commerce that generates wealth for us, during this important season of planting and initial growth we are serving others by generating wealth and opportunities for them as well. Our awareness in spring moves beyond mere ambition to seeking meaning in our work. The desire to experience meaningful events connects us more deeply with what we are doing and how we affect those around us.

In springtime, we leave behind passivity and jump into action. We stop being isolated and begin allowing synergy to occur. Instead of feeling constricted and closed off from others, we are open about our values, transparent and unrestricted by any fear that people will judge us negatively. We become expansive and develop a new sense of pride and purpose. The central question of spring is, *"What do I want to create as I go forward?"*

The gift in this season of the cycle is that new ground is laid for business to grow. With the debris cleared away, there is now fertile soil to plant in, allowing new growth, creativity, and expansion. In spring, we can choose to make a profound shift and create a new legacy. To do this, we have to raise our consciousness. We allow our compassion to arise as we operate with others differently than we did in the past, extending them trust instead of viewing their ideas and strategies with suspicion. Our relationships deepen and even feel more meaningful to us, because we're no longer operating on a surface level, pretending to be working cooperatively when actually we're just going through the motions, so we can get back to doing it by ourselves. We develop a new social identity, a new way to *be* in the world, based on a new foundation. Having already redefined our values and made a value stand, we no longer let fear dictate our attitudes and behaviors.

The risk of springtime is of slipping into stagnation and boredom, and becoming "disheartened" or even depressive. I can recall many colleagues remarking that they really had a hard time getting themselves to work that morning, or that they were so "over it" most of the time. This leads to individuals not feeling fully connected to what they are doing, or being fully invested in whatever the project or work at hand presents.

These are symptoms of people who are overwhelmed. They don't feel seen or heard, or as if they matter, which lowers their morale and productivity. The one thing I've learned from working with so many people overseas is that we're all basically the same.

- Everyone wants to be **seen**.
- Everyone wants to be **heard**.
- Everyone wants to be **recognized**.
- Everyone **wants to make a difference** in some way.

Acting bored and disconnecting from the mission can be a defensive stance that comes down to the need to be right, which is an ego distortion. However, when we overcome this, new possibilities open up and we can successfully construct a bridge between the old and the new paradigms. The transition within us is made possible by one simple, sadly unrated attribute: humor. We've all got to stop taking everything so seriously!

You're not always right. You never will be. You're a human being after all. Nor is everyone around you wrong all the time. Laughter and the general enjoyment of what you're doing will help to get you through the hard times, the challenging days, and the times when you are acting like an utter jerk. It is the way to avoid slipping into depression, feeling disheartened, and ultimately judging others. It will allow you to reach acceptance of yourself and others.

Optimism is the catalyst that leads us into the next season—summer.

Spring Summary: *The New Beginning*

Gift / Lesson:
- New ideas form, creative process begins, seeds are planted

Risk:
- Boredom, stagnation, depressive state

Antidote:
- Humor and optimism

Summer

Summer is a time when all the work that's been done in spring comes to fruition. With the emergence of new growth, our optimism increases and we start to perceive the many possibilities and opportunities open to us. The key question of summer is, *"What is truly possible?"* When an organization has been freed from its constrictive behaviors and has stopped compromising its core values, there is little weighing its people down. The potential for movement and growth is therefore tremendous.

In summer, there is little fear and creativity is abundant. Important elements, systems, and operational aspects from the old business paradigm in alignment with the new value system have been integrated. Business is flourishing, so secretiveness and unethical behavior are less likely to occur—even becoming foreign concepts to management and employees, who can't imagine a reason to compromise their values.

The gift of summer is the ability to operate flexibly, according to our core values, freed from the constraints of the ego and its past pathologies. Summer is a period of empowerment. We remain flexible and open to even greater possibilities. We planted and often discover we may now get an even greater yield than we originally dreamed.

The risk in this period is to begin lying and compromising one's integrity, core values, and authentic self to preserve the status and success of the season.

People lie in order to cover up difficult truths and to protect themselves from the judgment of others. But lies are like dominoes. Once one is discovered, other lies quickly become exposed. Ashamed to have been caught being dishonest, people will begin to shut down and then become secretive again in the vain hope of maintaining the illusion of power.

The core value here is trust. It is important for people to trust themselves, trust their internal guidance, and trust the process that they've cycled through to get where they are now. Knowing this cycle will repeat over and over again, they can commit to moving forward with diligence, because they've been through it before and they know the cycle is normal.

> ## Summer Summary: *The Possibilities*
>
> **Gift / Lesson:**
> - Flexibility, empowerment and unencumbered problem solving
>
> **Risk:**
> - Lying, compromising oneself in order to keep everyone happy
>
> **Antidote:**
> - Trust

It is natural to cycle back into autumn after the summer harvest, and it is better to do so consciously and with commitment, than to be forced into autumn by neglecting to assess our systems and results, or by a large-scale disaster. It is common to want to maintain the status quo, even if a particular situation could be better. But we do so at our own peril.

Cycles & Seasons of Transformation

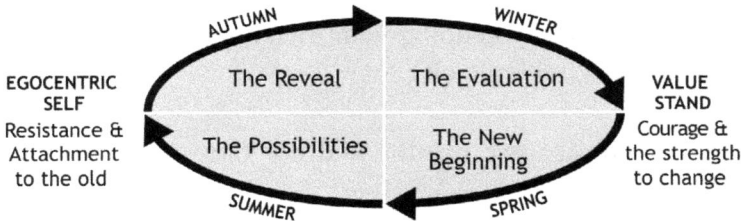

The Progression of Life and Consciousness

The cycle of nature serves as a wonderful guide for making both business and personal choices. Personally, I've found that when I'm aware I am in a state of winter, the action I need to take is making a *decision*. I need to decide whether or not I'm going to make a value stand and create new beliefs that are in alignment with them. Generally, it takes courage to make such a decision, but it's crucial for moving the process along. That means actually taking action. The action shows you have made a commitment. Without that commitment, the decision is meaningless and empty.

How much easier is it to make changes within yourself first and the organization second when you have a legible map! The scenic road is nice; yet why not take the shortest route to your destination? Do the work of the season you're in and do it with full-on conscious commitment. If you follow fear-based beliefs instead of making a value stand, you may find your new beginning took you to the wrong destination. Embrace the cycle of nature and you won't find yourself skipping all-important inner work.

Stepping back to observe and evaluate is something you need to do on your own as well as with your team, but it starts with you doing your own internal inventory.

Keep asking yourself:

- What are **my** results, and are they what I hoped for?
- What's really important to **me**?
- What matters most to **me** as I move forward?
- What is **my** real potential here?

Then, ask yourself these questions:

- What are the team's/the company's results, and are they what **we** hoped for?
- What's really important to **us**?
- What matters most to **us** as we move forward?
- What is the real potential **we can create together**?

If others do not feel as ready to change and make a value stand as you do, you can lead them. You can be a person of influence. Just remember it is not your job to change them. The most appropriate definition of a leader I've ever read is by John Quincy Adams. *"If your actions inspire others to dream more, learn more, do more and become more then you are a leader."*

By you yourself being different, by embracing new consciousness, you will activate the environment— stimulating new thoughts, feelings, and actions. Those around you will either come into alignment with your shift or they will simply leave.

This brings us to an important aspect of working with the seasonal cycle, which is the issue of *resistance.* In any season, resistance can rear its head and interfere with progress.

Resistance

Among important details related to the natural cycle in business, I've outlined the risk that's present in each season. This is the factor that's most likely to manifest as resistance to change and forward movement. When the leadership within an organization resists letting go of their distorted egos and the pathologies of the past, the entire process stalls. They will remain in the season until they come to terms with its lessons, or the business will perish.

However, it is possible and likely that you will cycle through this process quickly once you are aware of the potential pitfalls. If you experience resistance—your own or of those in your company—it does not have to stop you for long. Resistance to change is normal. It is fear of the unknown. Yet not all resistance results in destruction and chaos.

To transform your resistance into forward progress, simply assess where the ego is acting up and make the adjustment there. Hitting resistance gives you the opportunity to see another level of ego you may not have perceived prior. Resistance affords you the opportunity to further grow and open up your awareness as to what needs to change, in order for you and for the organization to move forward.

In life we're never "done," we can never expect to be perfect. Life is about constant growth, disintegration, and reformation. We must constantly raise our awareness, returning again and again to our authentic selves and expressing our core values in as healthy a manner as we can achieve. Each season has its particular purpose, and you can't rush through them if you want to achieve success.

At this time of upheaval in business, we are being asked to look at what got us into such a dire mess, and to evaluate our values and beliefs, so we can make new choices and move forward. We are being asked to return the culture of business to the bastion of integrity it once was: to earn profits while acting with integrity, openness, hope, trust, and creativity. If we say yes to this invitation, we'll be learning how to create commerce and serve others by creating jobs and opportunities in a different way. We'll allow business to flourish, nurturing its potential, from a higher consciousness.

With a new awareness, we can bring the seasonal process into the other areas of our lives as well, affecting not just those we work with, but those we know in many arenas. Our souls are calling us to create work with more meaning that takes us beyond merely generating profits right now and into a mutually sustainable system of growth.

Chapter 3

Make an Inner Shift

Meteorologist Edward Lorenz, who studied weather patterns, found that the gentle flap of a butterfly's wing can amplify many times throughout the environment and, over time, build momentum and sufficient intensity to create a storm on the other side of the planet. This theory is called *the butterfly effect*. It is the notion that very small changes made in a large system change that system.

The Butterfly Effect

Although it may not seem so, in any given moment, we have the ability to rapidly transform ourselves, and the world around us. When any structure falls into a state of chaos and the previous rules and general operating systems fail, it creates a domino effect, leading to a shift in consciousness. Even the smallest change within an organized structure can cause a rapid series of changes that make an impact on everything around it. Sometimes these are apparent. Other times it's an invisible accumulation over time. When you apply the butterfly effect to today's business climate, you see that one person *can* make a difference because we are all interconnected. Creating a shift is a matter of making a decision to think, act, and operate differently.

Every time wings flap, the wind will be moved, creating a gentle ripple in the air. The more you flap your wings, the greater the effect. The ripple of air intensifies as others join in, flapping their wings. What was just a simple value stand one leader made, acting from his or her most cherished beliefs, leads to an awakening and movement. You can make a difference wherever you are. It just takes one person to start the process.

The inner shift you make is to believe you **can** make a difference regardless of the fact that you are just one person, when you embrace the concept that we are all one. We are all an "idea in the mind of the universe," that is, the same energy force connects us all. When you take an action based on this new awareness, it creates a ripple effect—your surroundings shift. Your consistency and deliberate intent can create profound change in the world. That's how powerful you really are!

The Relationship Between Values, Beliefs, Thoughts, and Actions

To change within, you must become aware of your values and beliefs, as well as any beliefs you're holding that contradict your core values. For example, if you value honesty yet are secretive and act with a lack of transparency, such as not sharing pertinent information about potential business partners, you are behaving in conflict with that core value. Although you want your actions to reflect your core value of honesty, your fear of having your weaknesses exposed and others judging you negatively becomes your overriding motivation.

You have to be strong enough to look at your behavior honestly. You need to face the contradiction between your core values and your behavior. Then you must make a value stand, and choose to change the beliefs that violate your core values, that is, the values that reflect spiritual truths, not the false values generated by your ego.

If you make a value stand, you can bring your thoughts into alignment with your core values. This will change your actions and yield different, better results. Otherwise, whatever steps you make toward positive change will be impossible to maintain, because your inner thinking will not be in sync with your core values. Your actions and results will be out of sync with them as well.

You may not be fully aware that your beliefs contradict your core values, that they are rooted in the values of the fearful ego. For instance, you might think you value integrity and honesty. At the core, you do value them. You may believe that as a leader in your company, you should act with integrity and honesty and encourage others to do the same. But if you quietly hang on to a competing belief, such as, *If I act with integrity and honesty, I won't get ahead and we won't make enough profits,* you have an inner conflict. That belief is connected to the false values of the ego, which is ruled by fear.

You can't make a value stand until you discard the beliefs based in fear and a scarcity mindset. When you believe, *I am able to act with integrity and honesty, and lead my team into achieving excellent financial results,* your thoughts, motivations, and actions will shift. They will align with your values and you will start seeing results that reflect the sense of abundance you feel inside. Because your thoughts determine your behavior, you must shift your thoughts if you want any changes you make to last. Making an internal shift can result in a dramatically different way of operating in business. The status quo is no longer working and a shift is necessary.

Making a Shift in Your Thinking

A few years ago, I converted to a Mac computer. For me, this is a superior product. And I love the advertising campaign that tells me it's a creative tool, it's intuitive and it's easy to use. One of the lovely "dudes" in the store hooked me up with a crisp, new laptop and showed me how to make the conversion from PC to Mac using bridging systems (Microsoft Word, Excel, PowerPoint, and so on). I was thrilled! I thought, *This is so easy!*

I got home and immediately set up my mailboxes and transferred the documents I needed from my dying PC. Over the next few weeks, I fell in love with my Mac. It's so sleek, so sexy and trendy. But have I used anything other than the three or four systems I'd carried over from my PC days? No. I didn't even bother to read the manual to set it up! In that regard, I'm very typical. I am set in my routine and here I was, in possession of a fantastic device that can do much more than my old computer could, but I wasn't tapping into a fraction of its potential.

I had no clue about the power behind this little box and what it could really do to enhance my work and my life.

One day, I decided to buy the $99 One-on-One Personal Training program so I could learn how to unlock the secrets inside my new Mac. Within a minimal amount of time, I was creating video clips and comic strips, mixing my own music, and even touching up photos. My resulting presentation slides are really amazing. Organizing my life has become so much easier too. I had no idea this machine was so powerful and had so much potential! I had no idea it could create so many fun things that give me pleasure and satisfaction.

But once someone showed me how to use the basic operating system programs I was unfamiliar with, I was off to the races. Today, I love finding new ways of doing things on my computer. Who knew all of this was possible? Not me! Because I didn't know what the system was really capable of until someone explained it to me.

That's similar to why you're here. You're meant to discover how to use the most amazing tool for making any kind of shift: the mind. Until you realize how amazing a tool your mind is, you'll continue to operate in your old ways, according to your routines, and you'll unconsciously create a reality you don't want. You may say you want to change how your team operates, but you'll find it never happens.

Remember, everyone has a brain (although it may not always seem that way). Within this fascinating tool, you can change yourself and then, because you've changed yourself, you can transform your organization. You can take advantage of the butterfly effect. This is the mechanism for breaking free from the current paradigms of "business as usual" and the old business model that uses fear as the main motivating tool.

Your mind is extremely powerful, so powerful it can move and change things immediately. Most people have no comprehension of the mind's capabilities. As I discovered with my new Mac, if you choose only to run the same programs you always have, you will never know how much of your potential you're overlooking.

To make the most of that potential, you must understand two important universal laws that affect your abilities. They are the law of cause and effect and the law of reflection.

Chapter 4

Two Universal Laws That Lead to Change

T he butterfly effect plays out in two ways, through the law of cause and effect and the law of reflection. When you understand how these two laws of the universe affect your ability to make changes, you can use them to create the results you want.

The Law of Cause and Effect

Every effect has a cause. It's a law, like the law of gravity is a law. We look at the results in our lives and wonder, *How did I get here? How did I end up in this situation?* We don't realize we're the ones who directed ourselves. Our results stem from a cause-and-effect sequence that's easy to remember by the acronym TAM:

> **T**houghts
> *lead to*
> **A**ctions
> *lead to*
> **M**anifestations (aka results)

Your thoughts reflect what you believe to be true, and, as I've explained, you want them to be in sync with your core values, not the fear-based values of your ego. What you believe and value sets up your motivation for every single action you will take. There is no way around it. You can only act on what you believe.

Since your beliefs and values are housed in your subconscious, often you're not even aware of them until something occurs that brings them to the surface. You have been mentally and emotionally conditioned since you arrived on this planet, influenced by the outside forces of your environment, including your parenting, generational conditioning, cultural elements and experiences to which you've assigned specific meaning.

A single thought is so powerful it will determine your actions. Why? It is your motivating factor. You simply cannot take any action that is out of alignment with your thoughts. Your actions produce your results. TAM is a chain reaction, with your thoughts as the cause and the results (manifestation) as the effect. The universal law of cause and effect dictates that your results were caused by something, and they were—your thoughts created them. This means you cannot blame someone else for your results. You are responsible, no one else.

Understanding the simple process of how your thoughts create any specific result in the world is the first step to beginning to grasp the sheer magnitude of the power of your mind. With this awareness, you can begin to recognize why you've achieved the results you're seeing. It gives you the ability to become what I call a "psychic detective." The purpose of the hunt is to discover your underlying thoughts and beliefs. The point is not to create feelings of guilt for having the "wrong" thoughts, but to realize you have the ability to achieve different results. If you're experiencing drama, you can create peace. If every day feels like a struggle, you have the potential to experience ease. You can choose joy over pain, acceptance over frustration, and a future of hope rather than despair.

Because thoughts are so powerful, you need to pay attention to what your thoughts are and alter them if they're out of alignment with your core values. Can a thought rooted in the subconscious be changed? Absolutely, but first you have to become aware of that belief that's motivating your actions and leading to a specific result. Then you have to change your belief to one that is in sync with your core values.

Changing your beliefs sometimes takes a leap of faith. For example, someone who has never swum in his life may have fears and doubts about getting into the water and trying to swim. If he does climb into the pool, it's because he's told himself he is capable of learning to swim. He has changed his belief—*I can't swim*—to a new truth—*I can learn how.* Rather than becoming embroiled in fear of the unknown, and panicking, he has shifted his belief. He now has a new value, which is "being teachable and open to an opportunity."

To understand why you're operating the way you are, remember the TAM sequence. Your values are your *thoughts* that lead to *actions,* which in turn lead to *manifestations*. You will only act upon what you value, that to which you are emotionally attached. Understand the power of your mind creates your actions, which form your results, and you'll have insight into all the relationships you're in and why you're in them, including your relationships with your managers and your team. Recognizing the power of your mind is the key to unlocking your ability to be a change agent.

Are you willing to let go of your fear and play that role?

The Law of Reflection

Take a look at what you've manifested. Perhaps you're working with a dysfunctional team that refuses to cooperate, resists authority, and is defiant or complacent. Maybe your work environment is so thick with tension you could cut it with a knife. If you look around, you may see only hopelessness and despair, and you may feel a general sense of defeat permeates the air. Toxic attitudes and environments actually have a smell, one that's hard to describe—but if you've been in a poisonous work atmosphere, you know exactly what I mean.

Whatever you put out into the world will be reflected back to you. So if your environment is negative in any way, it is merely a reflection of your internal beliefs, thoughts, and values. This is a tough pill to swallow for most people. You might think, *How can you say I created this ridiculous economic state? How can you believe I would permit the slashing of my team and the loss of jobs?* I've had clients and colleagues ask these very questions in heated and emotional ways. On a large scale, it is not *solely* you who created your current situation. However, many minds thinking alike, at the same level of consciousness, have manifested these particular results.

What has been your role in creating the situation? You may not have participated in any kind of ego-based behaviors, but if you looked the other way and didn't say anything about the values, actions, and results, you were part of the underlying problem.

Before you dismiss your role in creating the environment in your workplace, take a careful look around you. The behavior of the people who surround you is mirroring and magnifying the climate inside of you. This may be painful for you to see and accept, but it is the truth. If you're observing complacency in a colleague and you feel a sense of disdain or disgust, potentially this exists within you too. You may express complacency in a slightly different manner, but you experience it and create results that reflect this trait.

For any leader, it can be excruciating and maddening to deal with certain personality traits in those they manage. But these people have been put into your environment to give you an opportunity to grow, to see what it is in yourself that must change, and to help you find the courage to make that change. They are reflecting back to you every wart, pimple, insecurity, and fear you have, and set off emotional responses inside of you that you'd rather keep hidden. They will show you your Achilles heel, the most vulnerable, softest spot. And yet they will also show you your greatest strengths and attributes. Both ways they will be showing you *your* motivations, the beliefs that drive your actions.

Years ago, I worked with a man who always blamed everyone else for whatever went wrong. It used to drive me insane. There were days I wanted to just scream at him, "Stop being such a damn victim!" He acted like a martyr and felt sorry for himself all the time. Perceiving himself as a victim allowed him to garner negative attention, although he was completely unaware of doing this.

When I thought about it, I realized the man was showing me that I was also feeling like a victim. I blamed my boss for not getting the funding for new staff we desperately needed, rather than being resourceful and creative in resolving the problem another way. I spent too much time walking around complaining rather than being proactive and finding a solution. My mantra was, "Poor me, pity me." My self-pity was a way to gain attention and recognition.

My coworker taught me a valuable lesson. By observing what he was doing, I became aware that I was acting out my own version of his behavior. Noticing how unattractive and unpleasant his attitude was made me stop and correct myself. As I moved away from my own victim and even martyr-like behaviors, the people around me followed suit. In a very quiet way, we shifted from a value system of fear (victimization) to one of taking personal responsibility (empowerment). There were no brass bands or banners that said, "Congratulations! You're no longer a victim!" Without drama, we took personal responsibility for finding creative solutions.

As they reflect back to you your own inner state, the people you work with will help you discover the answer to each of these questions:

- What behaviors do I find *acceptable* in others and myself?
- What is my *motivation* for everything I do?
- What do I *value most?*

In this example, do I value the position of being a victim and find this an acceptable behavior? Does this position provide me the attention which then becomes my motivation to be acknowledged—no matter in what light that may be? Am I valuing that attention and creation of drama more than the peacefulness of resolution? Is that the value I am holding onto? Don't be surprised if it is. Even though many of us would deny such a motivation. However, if you are repeating this pattern or any other pattern, it really is the truth of what motivates you and what is most valuable to you.

Often, there's a contradiction between what truly matters to you (that is, your core values) and what your beliefs are. Beliefs can spring from fear, such as the fear that there isn't enough to go around. When you're in a scarcity mentality, it's easy to start believing, *I'd better get mine, right now, because very soon, there's not going to be any more.* If you're feeling a sense of panic, you're likely to go into a survival mentality and focus on what you think you need in the short-term, rather than what you want to create in the long-term.

When you're feeling fearful, you create situations that mirror that fear. The law of reflection explains why our inner world and outer world look so much alike. If you're not happy with the situation in your organization, look inward. Perhaps you've had a disgruntled employee utterly defy your requests to perform a task in a certain way. Could this person be reflecting back to you your own defiance, your own need to be in control, or possibly, your own frustration at being controlled by someone else? There are many possibilities. Think about how his or her behavior might be reflecting something inside of you—perhaps something you don't like to acknowledge.

The flipside of the coin would be a situation where someone you work with is reflecting something positive within you. Perhaps you've been touched by the commitment and tenacity of a colleague. Maybe he has an unflappable belief in what he is doing and what he can bring to any given situation, and you admire and value his faith and confidence, and wish you had these qualities, too. It could be that he is reflecting the highest elements and attributes inside of you that you may or may not be aware of. Sometimes, our best inner qualities are dormant and are shown to us, so we can make a choice to move forward or recede into the background of hopelessness and despair around us.

Each interaction with others in your organization will show you something about yourself and your abilities and motivations. But what about the bigger picture?

How we engage in business affects the economy and society. One has to wonder what was "acceptable, motivating, and valuable" to the leaders in the many businesses collapsing around us. Did we somehow create this catastrophic environment? Are we responsible for the perceived deceit and selfishness in the world today? Have we contributed to the breach of trust we've seen? I believe that you are, and I am. We all are. The reckless use of company funds, the exploitation of people and resources, and the pursuit of profits at any cost were a reflection of a dysfunctional value system that collectively underlied our thoughts, actions, and manifestations.

Since the flaws in the business world were revealed (autumn), now we are being asked to evaluate what is really important (winter). It's time we make a commitment to a different choice (a value stand), so we can move forward to a new way of operating in business (spring) and bring back the desired results of profitability as we operate collaboratively and creatively (summer). To do this, first we must all distinguish between the values and beliefs rooted in the higher self versus those rooted in the ego. This will help us figure out what we want to plant come spring.

Chapter 5

Two Minds That Don't Think Alike

Within your magnificent super computer of a brain there exists two separate and distinct minds that are diametrically opposed: They are the *ego self* and the *higher self*. Let's take a look at how they're different.

Your Two Operating Systems

Of your two minds, one is optimistic, hopeful, creative, and open to something new. The other insists you're a fool for even entertaining the notion of hope and positive change. One firmly believes that what you have to offer your business and the world is of great value. The other is afraid you're worthless and inefficient. You may try to be positive, forward-looking, and innovative, but in a split second, the other mind can take over and drag you back into feeling fearful and pessimistic.

The fearful ego self struggles for control of your actions and results. It does not trust the higher self to guide you. It creates the endless chatter in your head and thoughts that are rooted in its fear, motivating you to act in ways that maintain the status quo at all costs, rather than strive for something better. Its main power lies in its ability to manipulate and control the mind, edging out the thoughts and beliefs of the higher self. When we identify with the ego self, we try to manipulate and control others by using fear, and yet we ourselves are controlled by our own fear!

The ego, in the way we will refer to it here, is based on the Greek translation of the word *ego:* a separation of the self due to false beliefs about who we are. Who are we? All of us are divine by nature and interconnected. We are capable of operating with unconditional love for others and ourselves. The higher self knows this to be true.

The separation between the higher self and the ego takes place on two levels:

- The separation of the ego and the higher self within the individual
- The separation of the individual from God or the Spiritual Source

The Ego Self

The ego self operates from a base of fear, which fuels and perpetuates feelings of lack and insecurity. A perception of lack causes feelings of insecurity, while feelings of insecurity cause the perception of lack. It's helpful to envision this relationship between fear, lack, and insecurity as the three sides of an equilateral triangle.

Ego Self Model of Consciousness

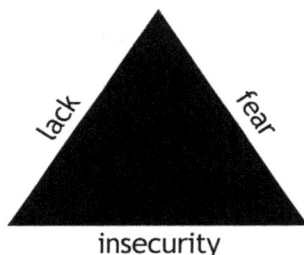

In nature, the strongest structure is an equilateral triangle. Each side of the triangle is the same length. Each side is dependent upon the other two to keep the form intact. If you shifted any part of the triangle, it would slide and eventually, completely collapse. However, the weight of the equal sides creates a leveraging system that allows the form to be nearly indestructible. All sides support the others.

When stuck in the triangle of the ego self, we experience fear, insecurity, and lack, which lead to greed, competition, judgment, character assassination, addictive behaviors (sex, drugs, alcohol, food, and so on) selfishness, doubt, drama, and individuals jockeying for position. Every day becomes like an episode of *Survivor*, where thirty people are left in the wild to compete for resources. Only one can win the game. Fear is such a powerful tool for influencing others that it's used in advertisements, political campaigns, and business strategies. Today, the media seems to spend excessive amounts of time finding new ways to evoke feelings of fear in people in an attempt to boost ratings, further encouraging this mental state. Some organizations use fear to motivate their sales forces or to manipulate employees to operate from a fear that if they make any changes or deviate from the status quo they will jeopardize the bottom line.

A fear-based mindset generates beliefs such as, "The market is tough and we have to fight fiercely for our share of it" and "We can't try something new unless we're absolutely certain we won't lose any customers or profits." When identifying with the ego self, our decisions are based on survival rather than the collective whole. Our individual ego convinces us, *I have to look out for me and me alone.*

When an organization or team is operating from the ego self, the attitude is, "We have to be number one at all times and how our actions affect others isn't our concern." The ego self has a very primal mindset steeped in ancient beliefs about "surviving" rather than about "thriving and growing." Its primary focus is "I" rather than "we."

The ego self is concerned solely with its own satisfaction and with "saving face." Nothing beyond that really matters because to the ego, there is nothing beyond itself. It leads a person to not trust anyone or anything. This may sound extreme, but the point can be demonstrated in many ways, as you will see.

Someone who manages or leads from the ego self may project the emotion of fear onto others. Rather than feeling like the victim of hopelessness and despair, he or she will be the one to victimize or exploit the people around them in order to gain power and quell their inner fear. People are often unconscious of the fact that they're being abusive or that the fear of the ego self is at the heart of their behavior.

The FARCE Syndrome

There are five characteristics of the ego self that anyone can easily identify within themselves. Everything we have discussed thus far funnels into this one system called The **FARCE** Syndrome.

Identifying the Ego Self: The FARCE Syndrome	
F	Fear
A	Attachment
R	Resistance and/or retaliation
C	Control
E	"Everybody but me..."

We've already discussed fear at great length.

But where are you attached? When do you feel more attached to a specific standing you may have, a title or a sense of security that prevents you from being flexible and solution driven?

When have you felt resistant just to be rebellious or feel the need to be right? When has this resistance been used to spite another person from getting their way? Have you ever felt the need to retaliate against someone?

Does the very idea of letting go of controlling a situation make the hair stand up on the back of your neck? Does relinquishing control make you feel unsafe and a little freaked out?

Have you ever looked at others with envy and thought they had an unfair advantage to success? Or simply thought you would never have the opportunities others have/had so why bother? Has the self-pity ever felt so overwhelming you couldn't see the possibilities or opportunities in front of you?

These are the symptoms of the ego that tells you to search for what you want, but it will never be fulfilled or accomplished. They are the defenses against progress and change. Oftentimes providing the need for self-preservation above everything else. They are the hurdles and challenges I highlighted in the transformational cycles and seasons model that can stop your forward progress. The ARCE all dovetails right back into the overarching concept of F for Fear: lack and insecurity.

The FARCE Syndrome in Action

Mark was an ambitious man who worked in a family-owned business for more than fifteen years. He climbed his way up the ladder and, when the founding partners decided to retire, Mark was tapped to run the largest portion of the business within the company.

They designated another man, Wes, to run the other portion. Mark took a business that was very profitable and within two years, it was limping along. He operated under the "What have you done for me lately?" premise. One day he would hire the bright shining star on the horizon, but the next day he would fire him, impatient with the lack of immediate results. He ruled with an iron fist and demanded that his own selfish whims be indulged over the priorities of running the business.

The staff feared him and when bonus time came around, Mark was reported to have grossed several million dollars yet he did not share the wealth with his team. He rarely bestowed bonuses, and when he did, they were minimal. Eventually, most of the long-time loyal staffers could not deal with his controlling ways and left. Within three years, the HR department was hard-pressed to find people who would work for this tyrant.

Mark's ego-based sense of lack and insecurity caused a chain reaction of fearful thoughts, feelings, actions, and results that reflected his internal reality. He created the very situation he feared: a lack of profits. He always thought his problem was a particular employee, product, or client, or the business climate, but the "problem" lay within him.

When you come from a place of fear, you can't expect any result other than lack or insecurity. Your sense of lack causes you to believe there is never enough: not enough resources, time, money, customers, or opportunities. However, if you come from a place of love, you believe anything is possible. Creativity, resources, opportunities, and solutions are everywhere. Your mind opens to a wide playing field of possibilities.

The actions you take when you are in a love mindset will yield very different results than fear. To achieve this mindset, you have to let your higher self be your guiding force.

The Higher Self

Within each person resides his or her divine identity. This divine identity is your highest self. It's the part of you that recognizes your connection to the world around you, and to other people. Instead of being concerned only with your personal survival, the higher self is focused on the greater good for everyone, including yourself. While the ego self is based in fear, lack, and insecurity—leading to pessimistic beliefs and a scarcity mindset—the higher self is based in love, compassion, and acceptance—leading to optimism and a sense of abundance and possibility. The higher self is willing to take risks and embrace change, because it recognizes change is an opportunity for creating even better situations.

Everyone has a higher self, but our perception of what it is varies depending on our culture, conditioning, experiences, the beliefs instilled in us by our family of origin, and other outside influences. There are three distinct characteristics of this divine identity operating within each of us at all times, even when we're unaware of them and unknowingly allow our ego self to dominate our consciousness. They are innate.

Just like the traits of the ego self, the three characteristics of the higher self form an equilateral triangle. In this case, love is the base and the two additional sides are compassion and acceptance. Compassion results in acceptance. Acceptance leads to compassion.

Higher Self Model of Consciousness

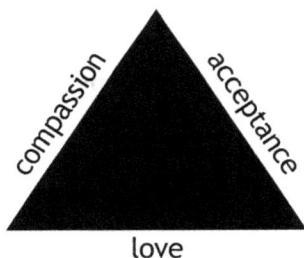

Love, compassion, and acceptance reflect the pure nature of Spirit in the world. They are interdependent and interconnected. You can't be compassionate toward another human being if you have no love for humanity itself. You won't be accepting of others if you don't have compassion for them, even if you aren't having the same experiences they are and can't understand their choices. Compassion starts with having compassion for yourself, which you can then extend to others.

When you operate within this triangle, you experience an overwhelming sense of peace, abundance, and support. You make your decisions with a sense of possibility and you feel secure, believing you're being cared for by the original source of your higher self. Your power is in your love for yourself and others.

As the Dalai Lama says: "Love and compassion are necessities, not luxuries. Without them, humanity cannot survive."

Even if the outside evidence seems to contradict this perception, when you are in a loving mindset, identifying with your higher self, you experience a quiet steadiness. You're accepting of your present situation, yet have the faith that it can be improved upon by using creativity to envision something better.

In a state of love, compassion, and acceptance, you're able to let go of fear and make decisions based on what is best for the larger group as well as yourself. There's no sense that you have to compete with others in order to achieve what you need. Instead, you trust in collaboration.

Because your higher self is open to possibility, it allows you to access your creativity. You feel free to express yourself and take risks, and you don't fear the judgment and disapproval of others.

The LAFF Method

As with the ego self there is an acronym to sum up the higher self succinctly. It is the method that brings together all the antidotes and catalysts from the transformational seasons and cycles model: hope, optimism, persistence, trust, humor, and even laughter are the working parts within the LAFF System. (Forgiveness is used in place of compassion because in order to have compassion, one must first forgive) It provides the foundation for solid long-term relationships with customers and staff, your community and your ability to do good in the world around you. All of this gets bottom-line results!

Summary of the Higher Self: The LAFF Method	
L	Love
A	Acceptance
F	Forgiveness
F	Forward motion

Love, acceptance, and forgiveness allow you to move forward. They foster the willingness to embrace change and counteract The FARCE Syndrome.

Using Your Higher Self to Stimulate Results

Remember Mark, the manager who let his ego take over and sent the fortunes of his company spiraling downward? There was another manager, Wes, who operated in a very different manner. He worked from a base of love, allowing his higher self to dominate his thinking. He treated everyone with the same respect and understanding he wanted for himself. Wes once said he never hired anyone unless he believed that person could exceed his expectations. He was ever-mindful of the bottom line because he knew the way to motivate and retain the best people was to share the profits with them.

To Wes, everything and anything was possible. He was a beacon of positive energy and made a habit of challenging everyone to really stretch themselves to find new solutions, create new avenues and streams of income. If you were in the office early you would find Wes sitting in a manager's office or an assistant's cubicle shaking their grey matter and making them think differently about any perceived challenge, as an opportunity to find something greater and more innovative that would contribute to everyone's ultimate success.

Every year, Wes would personally go over all the numbers in the business to ensure every person eligible for a bonus received one worthy of his or her efforts. He believed with all his heart that his people were what made him successful, and so it was only fair for them to share in the company's success.

Wes operated from his higher self rather than his ego, from love and compassion rather than fear and insecurity. Because his thoughts were rooted in love, he was able to achieve results that reflected love, compassion, and acceptance. He created abundance. Not only that, he was considered one of the most respected business leaders in his industry. People followed Wes. He inspired them. They learned from him and they aspired to be better than they were.

Chapter 6

Act From Your Higher Self

The concept of a higher self may seem like a fluffy notion, especially in business. We don't usually think of "love" as our bottom line. However, when you look at each mind, the thoughts it creates, the actions it causes us to take, and the results we achieve, we begin to see that having fear as our base doesn't lead us to where we want to go.

The Rollout of the Minds

Our old model of operating in business is rooted in the ego self. It wasn't always this way. Immigrants came to the United States of America (and still do), and achieved success by working with the fertile seeds of opportunity, hope, and a sense of abundance, all of which reflect the higher self. They escaped oppression and lack of opportunity in their homelands and were able to start anew here. Despite challenges, they believed in their potential, took risks, used their creativity, and built an even stronger country and thriving businesses.

But somewhere along the way—as often happens—fear took over. Business leaders stopped believing in the possibility of creating something new and even better, and instead adopted a "business as usual" attitude. The results it achieved are now crumbling. The current chaos can drive us deeper into fear, or it can be purifying and cleansing. We can allow the burning away of the old to draw our attention to our potential for planting something new. We can view this period of time as an incredible opportunity. In spring, all of the observing and assessing we've done gives us clarity about what we want to plant, what changes we want to make, and what soil we want to use.

In the corporate arena, as we move from autumn to winter, we experience the desire to plant something new. We've hit the point where, in essence, we've cleared out the old and now we are presented with the opportunity to choose a new way to be. The pressure is on markets and business leaders to shift out of the old, fearful, "survival" mode and into a new, optimistic, creative way of operating. Business today lacks innovative spirit. Companies and industries are stagnant and cannibalizing their resources and people. Without a reinvention or rebirth in the way we do business, we will continue on a course of chaos and breakdown.

Deep down, you know a shift is needed in order to bring about a breakthrough. It's time to plan and create a new, sustainable way of operating and resolving perceived "problems" by viewing them as new avenues of potential.

Businesses that are built on a model of chaos are completely unsustainable in the long-term. Chaos reflects the elements detailed in The FARCE Syndrome, the ego self. These elements can yield short-term rewards but rarely go the distance. The problem is when people hide the truth of what they're doing. For example, a company that had been praised for its large pensions, generous benefit plans, and effective management was Enron. For six years Enron was listed on *Fortune* magazine's "America's Most Innovative Companies" list. However, in 2001 it was revealed that reports of Enron's profits and assets were inflated, fraudulent, or completely nonexistent. It was one of the biggest corporate scandals of our day when the company collapsed.

How could this deception have occurred? Potentially, top-level management, operating from the ego self, created a chaotic business model that produced excellent short-term results, which couldn't be sustained. Instead of going through the seasonal process of evaluation and planting, so as to retain what was working and come up with new possibilities for generating profits, management chose instead to cover up their disappointing results. Survival and "what's in it for me?" rather than sustainability and concern for the larger group were their motivators.

In contrast, a sustainable business model is built on a foundation of love supported by compassion and acceptance. The mission is rooted in core values rather than pure ambition. An example of a sustainable business is Tony Hsieh's Zappos.com. Zappos is based on one core value: happiness. The extension of this core value is reflected in the brand mission to have the best customer service possible. Hsieh maintains that your company culture and brand is in fact the same thing. Therefore he has constructed the company environment to reflect this element of happiness within his team's working environment. His philosophy focuses on what he calls the "Framework for Happiness": perceived control, perceived progress, connectedness, and vision.

A focus on happiness as its "bottom line" makes for a profitable business that can expand beyond its initial profile of offering only shoes via Internet sales. Zappos.com now sells handbags, accessories, and more, to the tune of one billion dollars in annual revenue. The Zappos.com team has effectively blended core values, actions, and meaning in a positive way from the management team to the employees.

Model of Chaos

Ego Self Characteristics	Motivations and Actions	Manifestations / Results
<ul><li>fear</li><li>lack</li><li>insecurity</li></ul>	<ul><li>competitiveness</li><li>greed</li><li>controlling behaviors</li><li>perfectionism</li><li>self-centeredness</li><li>selfishness</li><li>arrogance</li><li>intolerance</li><li>exclusion of others</li><li>doubt</li><li>pessimism</li></ul>	<ul><li>falsified earnings and returns</li><li>Ponzi schemes</li><li>unfair compensation practices</li><li>smaller profits</li><li>self-centered decisions</li><li>working harder to maintain the same results</li></ul>

	<ul><li>a "business as usual" mentality</li><li>an unwillingness to take necessary risks or make investments</li><li>focus on the short-term</li></ul>	<ul><li>stagnant job growth or layoffs</li><li>slowed industrial development</li><li>diminished innovation</li><li>low morale</li><li>a competitive and uncooperative atmosphere</li><li>feelings of lack, fear, and insecurity</li><li>difficulty maintaining success long-term</li></ul>

The alternative, leading from your higher self instead of your ego self, means a different sequence of thoughts, actions, and manifestations:

Model of Sustainability

Higher Self Characteristics	Motivations and Actions	Manifestations / Results
▪ love ▪ compassion ▪ acceptance	▪ collaborating ▪ sharing ▪ giving ▪ social and global consciousness ▪ tolerance ▪ practicing acceptance ▪ forgiveness ▪ compassion ▪ respect ▪ exploring ▪ questioning from a place of curiosity and openness ▪ envisioning long-term health of the company and its people	▪ teamwork ▪ innovative ideas ▪ creative solutions ▪ willingness to learn ▪ large-scale impact (locally or globally) ▪ evolution not extinction ▪ higher profits ▪ job creation ▪ the emergence of new industries and new ways of operating ▪ advances in technology ▪ high morale ▪ sustainability even in times of crisis and downturn

A business becomes sustainable when its values are in alignment with the highest good of all concerned. To achieve this alignment, you don't have to roll out yoga mats and chant in the corridors (unless you want to), or impose a specific spiritual dogma on anyone. We all have a higher self that is focused on what is best for everyone, not just one individual (ourselves) or a small group (such as management, the division, or the company) versus the customers.

Following the seasons and cycle of transformation, working with its rhythms, allows us to clear out all the clutter so our natural core values can emerge. When we're clear about our core values and not giving in to the ego self—which wants to impose its false values on us—we are ready to write a proper mission statement that reflects this belief system. Once this step is taken, everyone within the organization clearly understands the code of behavior and expectations.

When your higher self is in charge, your thoughts, actions, and manifestations are in sync with your natural values. As you lead, others will follow. As you become a living, breathing demonstration of your highest good, others are more inclined to follow you in the same manner.

John Hope Bryant, CEO of Operation Hope, said: "Leaders give—followers take…Giving inspires loyalty, attracts good people, confers peace of mind, and lies at the core of true wealth."

Chapter 7

Give the Best You've Got

E very day, you're asked to show up as the best possible version of yourself. You are asked to embrace your divine gifts and talents and share them with the world. Daily, you hope to express your higher self to those around you. As you make the shift from operating from the ego self to rooting your thoughts and actions in the values of the higher self, you stop being a *go-getter* and become a *go-giver*.

Being a Go-Getter

A go-getter is always trying to "get" something. The act of "getting" is, in fact, quite selfish: "I have to get my share of the pie!" or "I have to get *that* account" or "I need *those* sales." Sound familiar? Read those phrases again. These are examples of the ego self telling you there isn't enough to go around, so you better get what you want—now, before it's all gone.

This attitude is based in the false belief that there isn't "enough" in the world. When you have a mindset of lack, you don't see that the universe is infinite and holds infinite possibilities. Opportunities, resources, and clients are always here because the universe is abundant. When you understand this truth, there's no need to feel fearful or have a mindset of lack. You can stop being a go-getter and, instead, become a go-giver.

Being a Go-Giver

Sonny Payne is neither a captain of industry, nor an entrepreneur. He is a panhandler I have seen almost every day in the subways of New York City for years. He is the one who taught me an important lesson about giving that I will never forget.

A few years ago, one night after work, I was riding the subway and Sonny Payne entered my car. Sonny had always been "my panhandler," a man to whom I would always make sure I contributed. But today was different. He was different. Everything was as it always had been for years and years—he walked through the car singing and asking for money.

He had a great pitch and a beautiful tone to his voice, and he approached the cranky subway riders with humility and understanding, saying, "If you don't have it, I understand, because I don't have it either." As he passed through the cars on this day with hat in hand collecting spare change, something welled up inside me.

I watched Sonny carefully. What was it that was different tonight? He had an ever-present smile on his face and he said his usual "God bless you" to anyone who smiled at him or gave him a few coins, balancing carefully as the train jerked sideways, moving forward. When he got to the end of the car, instead of walking through the doors to the next one, Sonny remained in place and rode all the way to my subway stop in Brooklyn, where he got off. This was highly unusual. My inner voice told me to make sure he was okay.

I ran down the platform to talk to Sonny, who was walking in the opposite direction. When I called his name, he turned and smiled at me as if he'd known me all my life. I asked him if he had enough money to eat that night. He humbly said it would be okay, not to worry about him. I knew he was hiding something from me, that he hadn't made enough money to buy himself a meal that evening. I handed him a bill from my purse and asked him again if that was enough. His eyes lit up as he told me he would be staying at a church that night and that not only was that amount of money enough to buy him something to eat, it was enough for him to help someone else pay for their stay that night, too. He proceeded to tell me how grateful he was to have helpful people in his life and how blessed he was.

I was absolutely stunned. This man seemingly had nothing. But Sonny didn't feel he didn't have anything. In his mind, he was rich, so he was grateful to receive anything more than what he already had, and eager to share it and celebrate his "success" with someone else, which gave him so much joy.

Despite all he seemingly lacked, he didn't have a lack mindset.

We have enormous amounts of money, resources, and power within our businesses, and by comparison to Sonny, most of us are far wealthier in terms of material goods. Yet, how quick are we to tell ourselves a story of all that we lack? How many of us feel we have nothing to share, but in fact who we are and what means we do have is so abundant? In trying times, we focus on the exterior situation rather than the interior climate. As you continue to shift your consciousness, choosing to alter your beliefs so they are in sync with the core values of your higher self, your interior climate *will* change.

I heard Marianne Williamson speak at an event in Los Angeles years ago. The takeaway quote for me was this: *To love and be loved is everyone's purpose.* She was referring to a never-ending cycle in the world: To love someone and to give to that person allows you to receive more into your own life. You don't have to be a *go-getter* when you can be a *go-giver,* a concept elaborated in the book *The Go-Giver* by Bob Burg and John David Mann. Give and you receive. There is no stop or start to the cycle unless you choose not to participate.

Trying to get something from another person—whether love, validation, recognition, clients, resources, or the advantage in any given situation—is a result of a lack mindset. The perception that you don't have enough expresses itself in your life and in the workplace. Give to others without a secret agenda to receive something in return, and trust you'll have what you need—that is, trust you'll have "enough" and more.

A little-known universal law comes into play here: the law of receiving. When you operate from "giving" at all times, you will receive all you need. You need not give with the proviso that you receive something back. If you feel a person owes you something for your good deed or generosity, you're not operating from your higher self. Instead, you are being a debt collector who keeps a running tally of what is owed to him and maintaining a mentality of lack.

When people are in crisis, they don't need someone who is being manipulative for his own gain and stretching out a hand, while keeping silent about the IOU he is secretly tucking in that person's pocket. Giving to get something back implies there isn't enough to go around. At the same time, a person who is in earnest doing her best to improve, learn, and be active in her work shouldn't be asked to trade help to advance herself in the company.

The universal law of receiving simply states that giving *precedes* receiving. When you stretch out your hand and give, the universe naturally gives back to you. This is the infinite flow of the universe. However, what you receive may not be what you expect. The law requires that when you give, you give without expectation and without keeping a scorecard. By doing so, you are demonstrating your inner generosity and assurance that there is more than enough to go around. The long-term benefit is that you will receive the same. Your "return" may not necessarily be in the form or means you thought it would appear, and it may not come exactly when you expect it to, but it will arrive.

Most people believe giving is only measured in terms of money, but there are no-cost ways to give through expressing and demonstrating your internal abundance. Your positive thoughts, deeds, service, encouragement, resources, opportunities, and kind words all have value to the recipient.

Giving makes you feel part of something bigger. You might not feel that way initially, because the ego self will protest that you don't have enough to spare, and that you'll suffer if you give away too much. But generosity is an intrinsic part of who you are. By reactivating this part of yourself, you awaken to your higher self and curb the tendencies of your ego self. The thrill is in discovering "How can I give today?" rather than "What can I get today?" Give because it is part of your divine biological programming to want to help another person without having a hidden motive to get the better end of the deal.

Give to others by sharing information about a resource with a colleague or friend to help her complete a project. Lend a hand to anyone who needs it, even if it means getting your hands dirty. Listen to others without interrupting, offering advice, or judging the situation. Nurture and empower others by reminding them of their resources and strength. All of these behaviors will strengthen your organization and boost morale, even as they inspire others to operate from the higher self as well.

On the most basic level, offer a smile to a stranger on the street. Say "good morning" to a few of the other caffeine-needy folks in line at Starbucks. Give a seat to a mother struggling to juggle her children on a bus. These things cost absolutely nothing but have such enormous value.

When was the last time you told a colleague or competitor about a plum resource? When have you passed an opportunity along to someone who would be a better fit for it? Have you lent a hand to another manager who was having difficulties in getting work accomplished for no other reason than to be helpful? These are little everyday ways you can be a go-giver rather than merely a go-getter.

In business, there are people who understand the concept of giving at a much higher level. They leverage their leadership to create opportunities for others on a community and/or global scale. These people understand that what they have—whether power, influence, or resources—are here to be used for the betterment of others. Bill and Melinda Gates, who together established the Gates Foundation, are wonderful examples of the giving principle intertwined with the leadership responsibilities that have already been outlined. The fifteen guiding principles for the foundation clearly show they understand the basic operational outline of being a go-giver instead of a go-getter: Use your resources to be of assistance to others. Operate with respect, integrity, and accountability. Partner with and collaborate with others who advocate for change.

While it may not be within your realm of influence to give to others on a global scale in the way the Gates and others can, you can give where you are—in your workplace and community. Giving is energetic currency, which has a greater value than any dollar amount.

Symptoms of a "Getting" Mentality

Here are the symptoms of a "getting" mentality:

- Are you keeping a scorecard and anticipating that you'll call in favors as needed?

- Do you give the best parts of yourself or do you give as little as possible?

- Are you operating respectfully and kindly toward yourself and others?

- Do you walk past others who are in crisis or need, and think, *It's really not my problem*?

- Do you engineer your resources to be shared, or do you hoard them?

- Have you set up a dynamic of competition based on staffers "getting" what they want?

- Would you help a competitor by sharing a resource?

- Would you help a colleague if he were in crisis by offering your time, advice, or skills?

- Do you start your day asking, "How can I help someone today?"

There are many people who will emphatically insist that what I'm describing is poor business practice. In fact, it is quite the opposite. I would ask those who disagree:

- What do you find threatening about this concept of giving?

- Why would being helpful to others elicit fear in you?

Most often, behind the resistance to giving and serving others is a fear of losing power or control. Generosity and trust can be a challenge to someone with a strong work ethic who fears he won't see the rewards for all his hard work, as he thinks, *Why should I help her? She doesn't deserve it!* or *She's doing quite well, she doesn't need anything from me!*

The reality of the situation is that when you open your arms to another person and offer her assistance, the same will be returned to you—if it doesn't come back to you from her, it will come back to you from someone else. There is a gentle flow of giving and receiving in the world. Abundance is infinite. If you choose not to participate in this universal truth of abundance, it will be more difficult for you to gain the help you need when you need it yourself.

Recently, when I explained this principle to an executive I coach, she replied, "Maria, that's BS. I help people, but no one helps me. I can't rely on anyone helping me, ever." As we talked further, I discovered she doesn't give with an open heart. She is stingy, focused on what she'll get back in return. As a result, when others have tried to give to her, offering assistance or support, her perception was that they were either mocking her or just being nosey about her problems.

She felt if they were offering help it must be because they wanted something in return—the ability to gloat, power over her, or something else. Because she held this belief, she was unable to allow others to give to her. Her own protective shell kept her from receiving all she needed.

Part of being a go-giver is being willing to receive the goodness and gifts of others who want to express their support. It sounds crazy that someone wouldn't be open to receive assistance from another person or from the universe, but it happens because people are trying to be in control, rather than trusting in divine orchestration. The universe is working behind the scenes to give you what you require when you require it.

Opportunities and support come at the right time, through other people. You cannot give with an open heart when you are unable to receive with an open heart. The two functions are intertwined.

"The decision to receive is the decision to accept" is the way *A Course in Miracles* describes this best.

Chapter 8

Become an Agent of Change

B usiness can be a sustainable entity that helps perpetuate the cycle of life.

Being a Change Agent for a More Sustainable Business Model

Never forget that business exists as a means to create jobs, opportunities, and resources for all. A business has to actually be profitable to be a productive part of this interconnected system. A profitable business employs many people and efficiently and effectively engages resources to support their mission. This breathes more money, jobs, and opportunities into our economic system. A millionaire friend of mine always tells me, "If a business isn't making a profit, then it's not a business, it's a hobby."

Freeing a business from the ego's model of chaos allows new growth to spring from the soil again. Without aerating the soil of these old beliefs, the chance of sustainability for the long haul is not possible. You cannot fix what you cannot see. You can only see the problems when you've taken an honest, straightforward look.

Competitiveness and fear strangle any chance of creativity, innovation, and collaboration. Your role as a leader in your organization is very important because the change starts with you. You are the one who must change before anything or anyone around you will change. A change agent is someone willing to take personal responsibility for themselves and the world around them, because they know they have been a part of creating that world. More and more employees at every level are realizing if they want things to change, they must be the catalyst.

There are twelve distinctions to being a change agent you can look to as a checklist to decide whether you are indeed one. Each leads back to embracing your higher self and your greatest potential.

The Change Agent Manifesto

1. You are **open** to new possibilities for yourself and for others.

2. You are (or are willing to be) **adventurous!**

3. You are willing to **release** your ego in order to build a more profitable future.

4. You **question** why rather than just agree with others.

5. You listen to your **intuition** before acting.

6. You **blend** a savvy business sense with your intuitive nature and creativity.

7. Your **passion** is contagious (and everyone tells you so!)

8. You are known as **fearless.**

9. You are willing to **be** different from others.

10. You are a **pioneer** (or wish to be).

11. You fully recognize that **playing s**mall does not serve the world.

12. You are concerned about **profits** for yourself and others.

As you look at the thoughts and values behind your actions and your results, you start to see whether your mindset is dominated by your higher self or your ego self. Are you focused on your own survival in a tough business climate, or on the wellbeing of your entire group? Are you making decisions based in your fear that you're inadequate or lacking, or in confidence that you have something to offer to the company and to the stakeholders?

Your Role as Leader

Culturally, we have forgotten the single most important element of being a leader:

A leader is a person who is in service to others.

While a leader may have many people reporting to him or her, the most important task of a leader is to coordinate all the resources available to create profitability and abundance within their organization. They are servants of those who follow them. I recently heard someone summarize the true meaning of service as the "willingness to find meaning in what you do, beyond just personal gratification or ambition." When service to others is the foundation on which you stand, your mindset completely changes.

Over the years, I had formed a partnership with a gentleman from Alabama who sold buttons. One day, I witnessed him demonstrating just how much he values the concept of being of service. He was in my office to discuss some problem we were having in Guatemala with a shipment. I waved my hands and told him, "Just make it right, Joe. I trust you to fix this problem." He looked at me with utmost sincerity and said, "Absolutely. Because when I give you what you need to complete this project, then I've done my job well."

This was coming from a multimillionaire business owner who to this day instills in his staff the value of doing the job right above all else. He feels his job is to be of service to others in helping them achieve *their* end result and if he does his job right, he will achieve the profits he desires. His motivation is not rooted in his ego self. It's free of ulterior motives.

Now, this man happens to sell buttons, but his company's product could be anything. The philosophy is the important factor. He has taken a value stand, his employees' values are in alignment with his, and their thoughts and actions flow forth from there. His company's results reflect his mindset. He believes he and his company have something of value to offer and that his profits will mirror that value, and they do.

To be a change agent and lead your company away from the old, unsustainable way of operating into a more sustainable and profitable business model, you need to embrace the true role required of leadership.

The Four Functions of a Leader

1. **Be of service.** You are in this role to be of service and facilitate the cycle of nature, by providing tools which create jobs, profits, and opportunities for all.

2. **Be a guardian.** To be a guardian, you have to be honest with yourself about whether your thoughts and beliefs are free of the motivations of your ego self. You must be willing to keep others' egos in check, too, so the group's thoughts, actions, and results are in sync with the values of the higher self and do it without judgment.

3. **Give to others generously.** Be a go-giver in every aspect you can imagine. Nurture the highest good in all members of your team so they can reach their highest potential. Share your wisdom and resources

with others and be supportive.

4. **Consider the needs of the entire group.** Do whatever you can to ensure the rights of others are not violated in the process of building and sustaining your business.

When you find yourself doubting what you're doing and worrying about whether you're remaining too long in fall or winter, not moving forward toward spring planting and summer's flourishing of profitability, recognize your leadership for the magnificent conduit that it is. It is truly spiritual in nature and divine in purpose. You are one link in a massive chain that serves to change the lives of others. You are affecting not just the people on your team, or in your company, but the thousands of people who have jobs and opportunities because of your business, from the small deli that serves lunch to your workers to the grocery store where they spend their money. If you act as a change agent and lead your company into greater sustainability, you'll be helping all of those people to maintain the flow of profits and abundance.

Be a Courageous Change Agent

Not all leaders will be interested in changing or shifting the surrounding environment. Becoming a change agent is your choice. But if you've decided that the current way of "being" in business is no longer tolerable or profitable, and you're ready to make a value stand and, to paraphrase Gandhi, to become the change you want to see happen, you will need courage. You have to cross a threshold and leave behind the way of operating created by the ego self, then move forward into a new way of operating according to the higher self.

As you stand at this threshold of change, you have a choice. Fear and possibility push at you from either side with such pressure it can be difficult to make a decision, but you must make a choice. By making a value stand and transitioning to a new level of awareness, you can start creating beliefs based in what's good for a greater community versus what will benefit you and you alone, or you and your company but not others. You have to decide between serving "me" or "we."

This is the place where the rubber meets the road, where paradigms shift and outdated value systems are shattered. You are likely to experience a massive, cataclysmic tearing down of the old and ushering in of the new not just on a business level but on an individual, personal spiritual level. "It has been said that when you do the thing you fear, death of fear is certain. Courage is not the absence of fear and anxiety, it's proceeding in spite of them," says author Price Pritchett.

The reason the shift inside of you creates such far-reaching results is because by becoming a change agent, you challenge the illusions of the ego self, which tells you change is bad, that you must protect what you already have because you can't possibly create something even better. This is the stage at which you allow the dream of "What if...?" to propel you forward. It's the point where fear of being judged, failing, or experiencing retribution for daring can be stronger than your heartfelt desire to transform. That desire becomes so overwhelming you literally shake to your core to make that change. Your burning desire for change is pushing up against every fear your ego can throw back; this is called *a state of compression* and it occurs when you are being asked to make a decision one way or the other. Once you decide, the pressure is released. Fear dissipates. To move forward to make the decision requires faith that something greater than yourself will support you on this journey.

You may be experiencing this compression right now and feeling the pressure, as fearful or complacent people around you resist the changes you're trying to enact. Despite your determination, all the old fears of why the transformation you seek isn't possible will appear from the vapors to frighten you into believing that if you do something, anything, different, you'll be taking a crazy risk.

Thoughts such as, *What will they say?* and *How will others judge me?* may worry you. You may be standing in this place all by yourself, with no one supporting your value stand. If so, it is a temporary situation, so hold your ground! As author Keshavan Nair wrote, "With courage you will dare to take risks, have the strength to be compassionate and the wisdom to be humble. Courage is the foundation of integrity."

Make Your Value Stand

As spring approaches, you must begin planting seeds. In business, you need to make a plan and goals. You have to be clear on what you're planting and what you want to harvest. Are you growing fruits, vegetables, or flowers? What is it that your company is really selling? Is it a particular set of products or services, or is it something else, something larger and more meaningful? What is your mission statement? And how is that tied to your values?

In spring, when you're planning what to plant, the umbrella question is: "Who do you want to *be* going forward?" That question is open-ended and refers to the values of how you want to operate; the very values and beliefs that will be reflected in your actions of *how* you do business and the motivating factors behind them.

- Do I want to continue to run this rat race of competition? Is there a way to create a sense of balance and rid myself of the feeling that I'm just part of the rat race?

- Do I want to continue to allow others to have their needs and wishes compromised in order to enhance the bottom line? How can I work differently so others are not compromised?

- In what ways has playing it safe led to stagnation and even a loss of profits or market share?

- How might I foster my own wellbeing and the wellbeing of others at the same time?

- Am I more attached to the drama of the problem than anything else?

- What am I willing to do and not do to succeed?

- What are my real fears about embracing a higher-self business model, and is the payoff of change better than the payoff of not having to face my fears?

- In what ways am I allowing my own fear or someone else's to dictate my thoughts, actions, and manifestations?

- Although I've struggled in the past to make changes and not succeeded, is it worth it for me to give it just one last try before I move to Tahiti and weave baskets on the beach for a living?

As you answer these questions, you may well discover a new conviction to do things differently going forward. By embracing the winter process of assessment, evaluating what you've witnessed, experienced, and participated in (at times, regrettably), you allow yourself to move into the next season: spring, and planting new seeds.

Chapter 9

Choose Your Team

I n this chapter, you'll learn how critical it is for your team's values to be aligned with your own.

Identifying Motive and Self-Esteem in Others

Rita is sitting adjacent to me as we interview the next candidate for a position that has now been open for a year. I've become notorious for taking my time whenever I hire anyone for my team, and people are wondering why I'm so "picky," but I don't care. I know how important it is to have the right dynamic and chemistry, so all the wheels in our machine continue to churn peacefully and harmoniously. I have always been this way and it's served me very well throughout my career. I've rarely had to fire anyone.

One of the standard questions I ask in any interview is, "Who are you, really?" I always love the reaction I get. The recipient is usually taken aback, blinks several times, and ponders just how to answer me. I can see the litany of possible answers racing through their mind.

"Well, I am Joan," she tells me with a very nervous giggle.

"Okay, Joan, tell me who you are."

She blinks and starts reciting her résumé to me.

I interrupt. "No, tell me about you. Who are you?"

Finally, she understands the question. She begins to tell me about her character and qualities, revealing her underlying motivations without realizing it.

Afterward, as we walk back to my office, Rita turns to me and asks, "Why do you ask people that question? They never know how to answer it!"

I simply smile.

Rita says, "When you asked me that question a few years ago during our interview, you totally freaked me out! I guess I answered the question right because I'm here!"

We both laugh.

"Well, would you hire someone who tells you he likes to hang out and watch TV, who likes to sleep a lot, and tells you all about the fight he had with his significant other?"

Rita thinks I'm joking but I tell her I've actually gotten those responses and a few rather salacious ones as well. "Or would you hire someone who tells you he really loves working with kids, being part of the local softball league, or playing a musical instrument? Maybe this person says she loves to cook and makes amazing chocolate chip cookies, or is a dog person who loathes cats."

Rita answers, "Well, I'd hire the second person."

"Okay—why?"

"Other than that I know we'd have fresh-baked goodies in the office?" she jokes. She pauses for a moment. "I guess because it shows what type of person they really are."

Why Is This Question So Important?

The truth about that question is that it tells me an enormous amount about the person in front of me. It tells me what they most value. Whatever they truly value and are passionate about in their life is directly reflected in the actions they take and the words they speak. These values are their motivating factors.

Most managers I know hire people purely based on their résumés. If they have a pedigree, they are obviously more desirable. But what if you had two résumés that were nearly identical? What becomes the deciding factor? Many times I hear managers say they choose based on whom they like best. Well, yes, liking the person and feeling you can work with that individual is important. I'm not telling you anything new.

So what's so important here? It's important to select a team based on common values and motives. That's not to say everyone should be alike in a cookie-cutter way. You need a variety of different personalities and skills to create a balanced environment. Nor am I saying, for example, that if you are someone who values family you should hire an entire team of parents. Or vice versa.

What I am saying is that in order for your team to work harmoniously, you need to have a group that shares enough common goals to be able to work together efficiently and effectively. What you are forming with any given team is a *complementary people consciousness* rather than the *competitive people consciousness* that creates unease and fear. You want to have people who resonate with the collective mission and whose motivations are in alignment with that mission. As you're reading this I imagine you're saying, "Of course, that makes sense!" Okay, now make a list of each of your team members and list what motivates them. Each person may have a slightly different motivating factor, but if you have a solid team, they complement the people around them.

Is everyone in alignment? When a team is out of alignment productivity goes down. Confusion, drama, and resistance become an everyday occurrence. However, when a team is in alignment, this creates a natural laser-like focus toward achievement, cooperation, and collaboration.

Every leader will have a team with a different set of attributes. The shared qualities of many of the teams I have led could be quickly itemized as follows:

- **Passion.** They need work to be fun and enjoyable.

- **Team players.** Teamwork is important to them. They know how to collaborate with those around them without taking a defensive attitude.

- **Committed to excellence.** They're committed to getting the job done to the best of their ability because they value excellence in all they do and take pride in their work.

- **Free of petty distractions.** They don't indulge in excessive dramatics. They are not interested in gossip, backstabbing, and conspiracy theories.

- **Focused on profitability.** They gain satisfaction from generating profits and contributing to the bottom line.

Any team will naturally reflect their values to anyone who is paying attention. The power of reflection works in groups as well! Most importantly, the team must be completely functional and harmonious if they are to achieve their common goal. Their achievements and goals should be in alignment with and a reflection of your own, so you have to continually clear any ego debris from your own motivations, thoughts, and actions. A harmonious group, one in which each team member complements each other, is an efficient and profitable team.

Dramatic Distractions or Teamwork?

Going back to the interview I discussed with Rita, as I talked to the candidates Joan and Bruce I carefully noted whether they would make good team members. Bruce indicated by the way he answered the question "Who are you, really?" that there was potential for a lot of drama and conflict in his working style. He projected many of the ego-self traits of being a victim and not taking personal responsibility. His attitude was completely out of alignment with the team he was hoping to join, and that would have made for an unproductive working environment for those around him. This does not mean this individual could not have made a valuable contribution to the current team in some way. Yes, the dramatic flare could also provide some entertainment! However, at what cost to those around him?

The second candidate, Joan, indicated she was a nurturer. I could tell by her list of favorite activities that she enjoys team camaraderie. This quality was exactly in alignment with the group's values and motivations. After she was hired, this woman let me know when she was comfortable taking a leadership role and also knew how to allow others to lead when necessary. This was a critical factor in our decision to hire her. Perhaps some honing of skills and knowledge would be required, but both would be a wise investment in building the team's productivity. And the cookies she baked weren't bad either!

A team member or a job candidate's motivating factors may be well hidden, but they are in operation at all times. If you look closely, you can observe what is behind their thoughts, actions, and manifestations (results). This is the "raw material" I referred to previously that holds the greatest potential for change. It's important to understand that whom you hire truly does make a difference. When you simply fill a chair with a warm body, you often end up with a team member who has a lukewarm commitment and is unengaged and unproductive.

Rita's Result

After I explained to Rita why I ask people "Who are you—*really?*" she began to walk away, then suddenly turned back to me and asked, "What did I tell you in my interview? I don't remember!"

I smiled. "I don't remember your exact words but I remember you told me you were a passionate, committed person who is open to learn, knows how to lead, and knows when to let others take charge. You told me you were special because you just wanted to be part of a team and that means you know how to be in service to, and with, others."

In the three years Rita was on my team, she never once proved to be any different from what she projected in that initial interview. She acted on these core qualities every time. Her actions reflected her deeply rooted motivations. Over the years she developed into a topnotch leader and helped turn around the flailing business arm she took over, although at times it looked to be a hopeless situation.

What Motivates You?

What do you most value? What are the qualities you exhibit and have embraced? Are they higher qualities, or qualities associated with the ego self? What are the motives behind your actions?

If at your core, you embrace higher qualities, you can work well with others. You can collaborate instead of compete, creating the results you desire. Your team will always reflect your own values and motivations back to you. They will continually help you keep your own values in check, prompting you to realign with your higher self whenever you drift away from the shared motivation. These people will probably be some of the most valuable teachers you'll ever have in your life if you can look at it this way.

Are you in alignment with your team? Do they reflect your motivations? When people talk about you as a leader, do they say you:

- Are honest?
- Have integrity?
- Are forthcoming with details?
- Hold very high standards for everything you do?
- Are tough but fair?

Or do they say you:

- Are a bit of a scavenger?
- Would sell your mother to get what you want?
- Are in it for the kill?
- Are very sloppy in your work and shove tasks off to others?
- Are a @%#!#@@*!?

Each person will of course have his own perception of any situation based on his own beliefs about what is "right" and what is "wrong." And it is imperative that you do not let another person's approval or disapproval dictate your behavior. Approval-seeking as an inner motivation leads to unhealthy, co-dependent relationships. Not everyone will understand or appreciate your changes in how you are choosing team members and directing your team, and that's okay.

Listen to and observe your team to ensure they are in alignment. How are they communicating with one another? What words do they use, especially in times of conflict or confusion? Without giving in to drama, and remaining detached from any strong emotions team members are generating, watch to see the kinds of actions they take to achieve their goals. This will give you a clear indication as to which business model they are operating with: chaos or sustainability.

Gently correct as you go.

Chapter 10

From Competition to Collaboration

I was standing outside a vendor's office in Pakistan. We were making an impromptu visit to one of their facilities and everything outside seemed normal. Our office representative proudly talked about the possibilities of doing more work in Pakistan in the coming years. Their prices were indeed extremely competitive. "It's amazing the amount of intricate work you can do," I said. "It's a great opportunity for us."

He nodded in agreement and smiled. "We have very skilled workers here."

As we continued to chat, I noticed he became somewhat distracted and nervous. He quickly shouted something in his native tongue to a colleague who had joined him on our tour. It was odd, as an American woman, to be alone on one of these tours without a male colleague, so the office was taking particular care with me. The office rep, a colleague of his, an interpreter, and the interpreter's boyfriend had all joined me.

When we entered the facility, I could see rows and rows of machinery. All the equipment was neat and tidy even if it was ancient. But now, I spotted what they did not want me to see. It was break time, and on the floor three children were playing near the machinery. As soon as I saw them, the rep quickly shooed me onto the next viewing area. I looked up at him and could see from his expression he knew I'd seen the children. He nervously waved his hands. "Those are just the workers' children."

I tilted my head at him, knowing full well he was lying. "Do they work at this facility?"

He looked away from me and laughed. "No, no. You misunderstand. They do not work here."

I gave him a disbelieving look and we continued on our tour.

When we returned to the car, he pulled me aside and quietly said, "You cannot tell them in New York what you saw. They will remove their business from here. Do you want that to happen?"

I was stunned. "Why are you allowing this?" I asked him.

"You know Americans; they don't care what the cost is except that it is as low as possible. They don't care. The children are happy to have something to do and work. Do you want them to starve?"

My stomach turned.

"Is this not the American way? Yes?" He smiled and I wanted to throw up. I was speechless.

Upon returning to New York, I spoke with my production manager. He listened to my outrage and simply said, "We can't be competitive without making some concessions. Grow up, Maria. This is the way of business."

I couldn't believe my ears. It made me embarrassed to be involved in the exploitation of children for our own profit and gain. I'd sat at negotiation tables, so I was not naïve about how the dance is done. But this was too much, a compromise that was completely unacceptable.

I went to the CEO and told him what I saw. That facility was taken off our list of vendors pending an investigation. Needless to say, I received numerous nasty, hateful emails from the rep in Pakistan afterwards telling me I was taking food out of the mouths of children. I was shocked he would allow his own people's children to be exploited. It surprised me, but what was more surprising is that after being banned from doing business with us, he found a backdoor way into working with the company again. He plied a different production manager a few years later with the lure of better prices, profits, and recognition. They set up a "submarine" situation and had another vendor front the operation. It was very sad indeed.

Competition has spurred on innovation and creativity. *Who can make the best widget or dowel? How can we get this product to market faster?* Competition has indeed created new opportunities for people in business. *What technology is required to achieve these results? If this product doesn't work, how can we provide a different solution and capture this market?*

However, competition can be perverted and became competitiveness. In competitiveness, people aren't trying to do their best to bring quality products and services into the marketplace. Instead, they're trying to take something away from others, or get something before anyone else does. Competitiveness is rooted in the ego-driven belief that there are not enough resources, enough customers, enough profits, or enough time. To ensure ones position, attacking and crushing an opponent is the order of the day. Rather than thinking, *How can I do even better?* a competitive person thinks, *How can I crush my opponents? After all, that's the only way to get what I want.*

A sense of unhealthy competitiveness has led businesses and industries to resort to unsavory or immoral business practices. This attitude has caused people to increasingly sacrifice their values. Compromising your integrity has become an accepted manner of doing business and even a sport. Some people cynically laugh about what you have to be willing to do to get ahead. However, this fear-based, ego-driven approach is now being questioned because rather than enhancing business, it has stunted its growth.

The amazing thing about competition is that there is so much subtlety in how the ego facilitates it. You might feel tempted to hide your ideas from others until you can present them to your superior and achieve recognition, even though your team needs those ideas now, not later.

In this case, your focus isn't on what's best for the company, but on what will allow you to get to the boss first and undercut your team members by presenting yourself as the one person who can resolve the problems at hand. If you gain recognition for your idea, you may think, *Good, I won that round and left them in the dust!* Do you see how insidious this can be? How far reaching? How detrimental? How addictive?

I once worked in a company where a group of people was so secretive about what they were doing and trying to accomplish, that they wouldn't discuss their plans with anyone. They were afraid their ideas would be stolen, that they would lose power if they let anyone else in on their goals. They would launch projects and take on new accounts and not discuss them with anyone else. They had many challenges, but didn't have the solutions and weren't willing to turn to anyone else in the company for guidance or help. As a result, their projects failed. They valued competition over cooperation, and thought, *We have to do it ourselves, without letting anyone else know what's happening.*

That belief (thought) led to behaviors (actions) that resulted in (manifested) failure. Fearing failure, they created the very scenario they most feared!

When you compete, you look over your shoulder and backward instead of toward the future. You can't see where you're going.

If you can collaborate with others, there's a good chance a better solution, one with greater creation and innovation, can be born. Potentially, you could even create not just a singular stream of income but several, or an idea that could spawn complementary ideas, new businesses and/or brand extensions. However, when you focus solely on getting your piece of the pie and beating everyone else out, you miss out on these opportunities.

Accept that the universe is infinite in its resources and inspirations and you'll find you don't need to engage in competitiveness. There's no need to feel threatened that anyone will grab an opportunity away from you. You don't have to deploy unethical tactics, take advantage of others, or measure yourself against another person's accomplishments. There is really no lack in the world unless you create it for yourself by adopting a mindset of lack. Your mind is really that powerful! We are asked to be creators and collaborators rather than competitors and adversaries. It's more critical than ever for the business community to understand there is enough for all. A competitive mind thinks, *What can I take today?* as opposed to a mind open to innovation, which thinks, *What can I create today?* There is a big difference between the two.

Is competitiveness holding you back? Think about whether you're competitive in the office.

- In what areas are you competitive?
- Would you compromise your beliefs in order to achieve a bottom line?
- Would you violate the rights of others for your own gain?

These are important questions to consider. You can learn how to make your team or company competitive without resorting to fear-based competitiveness. For instance, not all competition is about the exploitation of others.

There are many ways unhealthy competitiveness can seep into an organization. On a day-to-day level, competitiveness could manifest as:

- **Infighting.** Teams may fight to gain control over any given situation, or take credit for a project or idea.

- **Gossiping.** Defaming others in order to reduce their impact or influence.

- **Withholding vital company information that needs to be shared with other departments.** Team members cease communicating important information in order to gain an edge.

- **Throwing others under the bus.** Pointing a finger of blame allows the leader or team to gain favor in the eyes of peers and superiors by portraying themselves as victims, or innocent bystanders.

- **Stealing or trading company propriety information.** Competitiveness can lead to financial, technological, or creative theft.

- **Compromising values.** Higher-self qualities and core values are set aside in order to gain a financial edge and/or recognition from one's peers.

Now, ask yourself: *Have I participated in any or all of these types of behaviors at work? Have I perpetuated these beliefs and encouraged them among peers and staff? If so, why?* Look deeply at your motivating factors. It will tell you which mind you're working from.

The organizing principle for the ego self is to search and do whatever it takes to attain a goal, but to never be satisfied with any gains or have enough. Yes nothing is off-limits: Harming the health and wellbeing of others, or performing a character assassination of a colleague is acceptable.

This mindset of lack triggers insecurity among the group members who begin to fear what will happen to them if they don't fully engage in competitiveness. A competitive group is not a productive group. If team members are constantly looking over their shoulders or being distracted by watching the moves of others around them, they're not concentrating on the business at hand, nor are they allowing any of their own ideas to emerge. This is an unnecessary drain on productivity.

There is absolutely nothing wrong with wanting to be the leader in your particular niche of the market. There is no reason to share proprietary information. Nor is there any reason why you shouldn't want to do something better or in a more efficient manner. However, when you start to take something away from another person or group in order to achieve your goal, you're engaging in an ego distortion that must be addressed and corrected. It's a limited, shortsighted view of business.

Collaboration as the Entry Point for Creation

Insecurity and the need for control prevent individuals from collaboration. Afraid others will recognize they don't know something, they won't allow another to come forward and express another point of view or possible solution. It's true your idea might be crazy or unfounded, and you should get feedback on it. However, insecurity doesn't serve the purpose that constructive criticism does. It doesn't encourage the honing of ideas. Instead, it's a vice grip on business that prevents badly needed growth. Operating in a complete vacuum is impossible and non-productive.

So many times over the years, I've reached a point of frustration when considering an idea or plan for something really wonderful. However, for the life of me, I could not figure out what to do next or whether my idea made any sense. In my earlier years in business, I would hold on to my precious idea like a life preserver, thinking, *It's mine!* or *Don't touch!* Many of my million-dollar ideas, dreams, and hopes would just wash into the surf and never be realized because of my need to be controlling. It also kept me feeling safe that I wouldn't be judged if my idea was not met with enthusiasm. This only further created a feeling of insecurity in what I had to offer and share with the world. It's a vicious cycle! It wasn't until I developed a higher level of self-esteem that I was able to recognize the importance of sharing with others.

But how do you take an entire group down that road to removing all their defensiveness? The solution is very simple. I recall walking into a meeting with a new team that was assigned to me. A woman, who later became my most influential mentor, was leading the discussion. As I watched them, I couldn't believe how transparent they were. They were free of hidden motives and manipulative behaviors. It was amazing, even magical, to watch her disarm those around her with loving acceptance. She made it safe for people to express themselves. She removed the risk of looking foolish.

She did this by accepting whatever they said, and listening to and considering their ideas even when those ideas weren't really feasible. I am sure there were times she wanted to ask whether the person offering a solution was nuts, but she never did. She allowed others to participate in the creative process of envisioning something new without fear of competition or judgment. She would gently guide them to other possible avenues of thought, thereby engaging them as problem-solvers not mere drones. As a result, they came up with innovative ideas and solutions.

Hearing people out is a simple and often overlooked solution to ending the stalemates that frequently occur in teams. When the brainpower, the actual talent within the organization, is frozen solid in fear it limits the possibilities that could emerge. People disengaged from the creative process and afraid to speak up are not truly invested in the outcome.

The benefit of allowing others into your creative envisioning process will help you to see any blind spots you may have missed or not considered, and it permits people to feel part of something greater than their one "job" or "role" in the organization. It helps promote a proactive approach to resolving situations, rather than placing a mere Band-Aid on the challenge at hand. It creates thinkers and problem-solvers who are empowered and participate in the process actively. They are more likely to make decisions and move forward with comfort when they are in tune with the group's overall plans. And, take some of the pressure off all decisions needing to be made by you alone.

Five Steps to Creative Collaboration

1. **Transparency.** Without calculation or hidden motivations, you simply say, "Here's my idea...what if....?" which is a potential solution or piece of it.

   Note: Do not move from Step 1 until there are a number of possible solutions to any given problem or challenge. Trying to figure out the "how" in the next step too early in the process will kill an idea before it has time to take hold.

2. **Refinement.** Taking the raw idea, you begin to ask, "How do we make it work? Is it feasible, possible, and profitable? Are there weaknesses in the idea? How can we make it even stronger? Where are our blind spots?"

3. **Remembering whom you serve.** What does the customer want versus what you want for him or her?

4. **Creating a "cocktail" that works.** Aligning the necessary resources and partners to put the idea into motion. This is a further extension of collaboration.

5. **Rights.** Will your plan of action violate the rights of others?

It is very important to spend a good deal of time in Step 1—the "What if?" portion of the problem/challenge-solving period. It's human nature to want the quickest, easiest answer. But at times it does take thought; consideration; a good, long shower; some music and what an old mentor of mine used to call time to "dream on it" for a little while.

A Bread-and-Butter Challenge

Many years ago, I worked for a company whose core product yielded enormous revenue. In fact, that product was the division's bread and butter. When one of my colleagues visited the facility that made this product, he realized the manufacturing process was creating an undeniably negative environmental impact. He was very upset and he asked me to help him come up with a solution that would allow us to continue to sell that valuable core product without hurting the environment.

His passion for resolving this ethical issue was infectious. I understood his concerns. I said, "I admire your conviction, but I honestly don't have a solution for you. I'm stumped. Why don't you approach others to see if they have any ideas? Let's see if someone can offer us another option."

By asking others to offer him insights and advice, he did, over time, manage to move 10 to 15 percent of the business out of the environmentally challenging method of production. He was able to set aside his ego self's need to come up with a solution on his own, in order to be competitive with others and instead, engage an entire community in a conversation about finding a better way. He was strong enough to let go of blame and frustration so he didn't feel powerless to make a difference. He believed in his ability to come up with the solution by using the tool of collaboration.

Competition goes far beyond the minor gossip in an office. It is a massive cancer in our society that prevents forward motion. Being transparent and collaborating with others is the only way out of the box in which we've placed ourselves. Letting go of the need to be the one who comes up with the solution (the need to be right) frees us to come up with the very best one. Now, I am not saying you should give away your propriety information to others. It's up to an organization's leaders to determine how much people should be sharing vital information with each other. But should you find yourself feeling like you're hiding in the dark eating cookies, not wanting anyone to have a taste of what you've got, it's a sure sign you're in competitive mode.

Time to check your ego at the door!

Chapter 11

Open to Creativity and Innovation

When I was just a newbie in business, I worked for a woman who would storm out of her office and yell at me, "I need a new idea right now! *Right now!* Whatcha got, kid?!" I would be shaking in my boots, barely able to speak a coherent sentence, terrified that no matter what I said it would be wrong, not good enough. I felt if I didn't come up with a great idea on the spot, she would think I was stupid. It became easier to hide than risk being in the line of fire.

Because I embodied the belief that I wasn't good enough or smart enough, she was unconsciously projecting those beliefs back to me. When she demanded instant creativity, I sure didn't feel creative and I certainly couldn't offer her anything of use. In response to my lack of a clever idea, she would simply say to me, "Ugh. You're so stupid I should just tie that notebook around your neck and send you out for coffee. You're worthless to me."

The Building Blocks to Newness

Harsh judgment and disrespect shuts most people down. Ask yourself, "Is this the motivation of someone who is feeling love and truly wants to collaborate creatively to find solutions? Or is this the motivation of someone who is feeling lack and wants others to calm the fears of her ego self by giving her what she wants, right now?" I think the answer is pretty obvious.

If you haven't adjusted your mindset and motivations, if you haven't taken a value stand and brought your thoughts into alignment with your core values, you won't be able to let go of the attitude of competitiveness and, therefore, can't use the elements of creativity and innovation effectively. Having the right mindset and motivations is a crucial building block for innovation.

Can you be creative and still be competitive? Yes, but when fear is driving you, you won't come up with your best ideas. Oftentimes I liken this to driving down the freeway spending more time looking in the rearview mirror, wondering what the other guy is doing and whether you'll beat him to the next exit. When you spend so much time looking behind you to make sure you're ahead of your competition, you're not looking forward, to something better.

What if in your truest potential you actually have something revolutionary to offer to the world, but haven't because you've spent so much time looking in the rearview mirror? In effect you're playing it safe and not getting truly innovative ideas out there because of your fears of being judged negatively. Being too conservative, taking only tiny steps toward change will yield, at best, tiny financial benefits. This is playing it small. "Playing small is safe" is what your ego will tell you.

Planning for Expansion

Mike spreads his Excel sheets across his desk and points to the bottom-line number. "We have this amount for the quarter." He points to a double-digit million-dollar number on his meticulously formatted document. "I am pretty sure I can get more dollars. But let's determine a plan before I go shake my can at the SVP's office." After so many years of participating in this type of dialogue, I am still amazed by the numbers that are nonchalantly tossed around the room. I gulp hard. But I feel reassured; because I know I'm working with one of the best business partners I've ever had in my career. Mike has a unique combination of business sense, logistical savvy, and deep respect for the creativity needed to build and sustain a business. Mike is all of that wrapped up in his "nicest guy you'd ever want to know" suit and tie.

We sit and run through the financial plan. Much money is delegated to the protection of core businesses. We haggle over how much funding is really needed there. After all, that's the "boring stuff," not the sexy, new stuff. Then we put in place a plan for the acceptance of new products and ideation for the remainder of the money.

Sheepishly, Mike says, "Maria, promise me you're not going to let the team go crazy here. We need to make some money." Mike knows I've got a dynamic group of big thinkers in the bullpen just waiting to be unleashed. "Remember, we want to make money!"

I laugh and respond, "Don't worry! I'll remind everyone that the product is not for them; it's for the customer and needs to be geared as such. This is business." It's important to remember that inserting creativity into any business does not mean losing touch with who your customers are and what they really want and need. At times any creative force can simply get derailed by not being in touch with their demographic.

Four years earlier, this business was run solely on the back of core businesses with nothing in place to ensure new business possibilities would come in. This shortsightedness had resulted in the business cannibalizing itself: The entire vendor base was pricing out for the same four programs, therefore monopolizing valuable resources. Customers were bored with what they were receiving. We didn't implement any new marketing or packaging. As a result, the people working on these projects became disgruntled and left the business.

These practices cause a business to implode. There is a progressive bleed out of money and resources. Is it any wonder that within any industry or market niche, when everyone is offering almost the same thing everyone suffers? The impetus to buy decreases and the market stagnates. This is why the season of spring is so important. Without planting new seeds—new ideas, new innovations—and moving into new business models and plans, summer will not yield much fruit. It is what causes previously stable companies to become extinct.

In business, it's wonderful to have others around who are excelling. You can learn from them, adopt their best business practices and systems for your own purposes, and more easily identify niche markets that are underserved. However, when a business fails to fill those voids and anticipate (and create) what those niche markets will need next, the flow of monies slows and then stops.

Increasingly, business leaders are experiencing "model envy": rather than leading their company to be innovative, they're piggybacking on others' successes, copycatting their successful models and focusing on their core business products and services, rather than moving forward and creating something new to sell. People are afraid to step up, and step out. The tendency is to hide from challenges and play it safe rather than risk failing. However, without "expansion" there is no growth. A competitive, fearful mindset will keep a company locked in this state of paralysis, which doesn't allow it to flourish.

Hershey's Chocolate: Innovation Over the Long Haul

In 1897, Milton Hershey attended the World's Columbian Exposition where he became fascinated with German chocolate-making machinery—so much so, in fact, that he bought the equipment on the spot. What few people know is that when Hershey began investing in chocolate, he was already a successful businessman and established caramel maker in Pennsylvania. However, he had the idea that chocolate, which was a luxury Swiss product for the elite at the time, should be made accessible for everyone. He promptly sold his caramel-making facilities in Lancaster for one million dollars in 1900. Then, over the course of a few years he developed his own formula for milk chocolate that could be sold in the American market. The five-cent Hershey bar and the American chocolate industry were born.

Since then, Hershey's has expanded their line to include Mr. Goodbar, Reese's Peanut Butter Cups (my personal favorite), Whoppers, Almond Joy, and various other confections and treats, such as cookies, gums, and mints. All of this sprouted from the ability of one man to pursue his idea with such conviction and passion that it spurred a completely new segment of business in this country.

He did not stop at one great idea, though. He allowed the business to create new and interesting products along the way. Keep in mind that this business was started before the Great Depression and survived that economic downturn by continuing to be innovative. If you've enjoyed a Hershey's Kiss recently, you know they've weathered the storm and are still here today.

Creativity and innovation are not reserved solely for the prospects of creating new businesses or products. They can be realized in almost any segment of the business. Using Hershey's as our continued example, in 1985, the Hershey Company was approached by Steven

Spielberg to use Reese's Pieces as the choice food of his star character in the movie *ET*. What happened next? Sales of Reese's Pieces jumped 65 percent once the movie was released. Product placements and endorsement deals boomed as a byproduct. I'd say that was a pretty creative way to boost sales, wouldn't you? By the way, you might be interested to know Spielberg initially contacted Mars to ask them if he could use M&Ms as ET's favorite food and was turned down. Unlike Hershey's, they apparently didn't see this was a marvelous opportunity to expose the public to their product in a subtle yet innovative manner.

Innovation as a tool for building business is not new but it continues to be an extremely effective one. At the time this is being written, Apple is improving its new iPad product. Droid was launched as an alternative to Blackberry. Others continue to innovate such communication devices and the "Ap" phenomenon as a platform for new eCommerce expands. Barnes & Noble is about to launch its new brand extension called Pubit! as the digital age is ushering in a new way to obtain, view, and digest books. The advent of services like Skype allows people to connect on a more personal level faster and more economically. Standing still is no longer an option.

The Expression of the Individual's Gifts

Any business is an expression of the individuals within that group and the gifts they can bring into the marketplace: their imagination and inspiration. If you're constantly copying others and your core items must compete against others', you're neither fully expressing the highest potential you have, nor that of the business vehicle you are driving. When you're unable to be creative, the ego self's fear, insecurity, and sense of lack are showing up and affecting your business model. These elements do not allow your business to be a sustainable entity for years to come. A sense of lack may drive the desire to innovate, but fear and insecurity prevent you from trusting fresh ideas that are offered. To step out into the unknown, you must access your courage, faith, and passion. That is how new industries, products, and services surface.

Symptoms of a Suppressed Creative State

Here are the symptoms of a suppressed creative state:

- Do you shut down others before they can express a new idea?

- Do you fear that if another person has a good idea, you'll look stupid or you'll seem not to be in control of the situation?

- Do you rely solely on historical factors to determine how to steer your business?

- When offered a creative solution or idea, are you more apt to push it aside, or find other partners to help you realize it?

- Have you set up a forum or channel to allow others to suggest or express ideas?

- Will you allow others outside of your team or division to collaborate on a new idea that emerges from your group?

- Are you willing to offer a new idea or are you paralyzed by the fear of rejection or judgment?

- Do you have a deep need to always be right and prove others wrong by dismissing their contributions, suggestions or ideas?

Suppression happens on many levels within a group. On an individual level, if you're unwilling to share your creativity with others, you will need to look deeply at this issue and uncover any feelings of insecurity and negative self-judgment. The fear of looking foolish or being judged negatively, or even harshly, will stop most people cold. Put that fear into a group dynamic and what do you have? Stagnation. No progression. A slowing down, or stopping, of growth and profits.

Now ask yourself:

- Have I participated in any or all of these types of behaviors at work?

- Have I perpetuated these beliefs and encouraged them amongst peers and staff? If so, why?

- More importantly, how can I adjust my thinking and mindset to be more in sync with my core values, so I can be more innovative and lead others to exercise their creativity?

Chapter 12

Is It Too Simple?

T he solution I am offering you may seem too simple. Maybe you don't believe shifting from an ego self way of thinking back to a higher self way of thinking will lead you back to profitability, nor do you believe it's possible or feasible to let go of competitiveness. In fact, the very thought of it may elicit a deep, visceral response. And the idea of working collaboratively to create might sound like just a bunch of New Age mumbo jumbo. How can making a value stand based in love, compassion, and acceptance lead you to success?

As human beings, we tend to make just about everything excruciatingly difficult; the human condition is evidence of that. Our ego self acts up again and again, serving up a plate of cold lies and illusions.

The rules of engagement must change. The unspoken law is that if you follow the old rules, you'll do well, and if you don't, you'll be cast out. Conform or face retribution. We've built a system based on a "what have you done for me lately?" philosophy, where the rule is "every man for himself." Such a system has rules and limitations.

Business has a disease. Its symptoms are low integrity, competitiveness, isolationism, a scarcity-based mindset, and an attitude of "give to get." For too long, corporate culture has been characterized by fear and a sense of lack. The long-term prognosis isn't great. Consider what Albert Einstein once said: "We cannot solve our problems with the same thinking we used when we created them." If the current business mindset facilitated the recent economic collapse, it must be discarded if we're to shift into a new paradigm and the healing of the corporate world.

The prescription for healing is simply a return to your higher self, that divine self that resides within every single person. When you make this return, you embrace love. New beliefs, actions, and manifestations will flow from there. It's really that simple.

We are thinking, creating beings with untapped potential, and we're on this earth to do something wonderful. The current crisis in business is merely a reflection of how far we've strayed from our true identity and core values. If we have created this chaos by operating from the ego self, what would happen if we instead operated from the higher self? What would happen in the world? Is it possible that people would treat one another with respect? Could it be the dawning of a fairer distribution of wealth and resources? Is it possible that completely new businesses and industries would spring into existence?

"But If I Lead, Will People Follow?"

Doubts, fears, and concerns will always arise like hurdles in front of you, and you'll need to jump over them one by one. One of the main doubts you may have is whether anyone will follow you as you embrace this new way of thinking and being.

People will follow what is called a "person of increase," that is, a person they think has something they want. If you're true to your core values and you express your gifts in the workplace, your attitude will be infectious. Radiating a sense of peace and authenticity are the keys to attracting others and inspiring them to follow your example. It should not be your goal to "get" them to follow you. You need only be a person of increase and invite people to accompany you on this journey. It is their choice to follow or not. You cannot, nor should you try, to change or control anyone.

My experience is that at first it will take time to bring people on board, but eventually they will change their thought processes and follow your lead. Those who decide to continue operating from the ego self will usually come to recognize they either have to change or move on. Often, they make the choice to go elsewhere.

Just because you express love, compassion, and acceptance does not mean you're a doormat. The characteristics of the higher self also include assertiveness, truthfulness, and—sometimes—tough love. You can offer constructive criticism and be deliberate in your words, because you have clarity about what you value. There will be no disconnection between your values, words, actions, and results. Bear in mind that the changes you're making won't always be received well by the people in your organization. Gloria Steinem pretty much sums it up: "The truth will set you free. But first, it will piss you off."

Oftentimes we are taught all it takes to make any change is to make the decision to do so. However, making the decision without the commitment to take the necessary actions, hold tight during the storms (and it will storm), trials, and tribulations until the momentum ultimately creates the shift, is empty. It is about really making this commitment to yourself first, then the ripple effect will intensify and build as you flap your wings.

Always Check Your Own Motivation

Whenever doubt, fear, or anxiety come into play, it's time to check on what your mindset is, and whether your beliefs are contradicting your core values. Whenever you have the slightest inkling that your actions and words may be ego-based, it's time to pause for a moment and be honest with yourself. Ask yourself:

- Why am I doing this?
- What am I doing this for?
- What am I trying to gain?

If any of the answers shows you're playing by the old rules, you need to jump off that speeding train as fast as possible. Never forget that the highest purpose of business is not to boost the bottom line, increasing profits as quickly as possible but simply to *perpetuate life, give others opportunities, provide resources, and regenerate, so the business is sustainable and profitable in the long-run.* These things come as a result of achieving profits.

Achieving these goals should be your motivation, and your role is to be one of the catalysts that aids in this process. You're providing a service that helps others to have jobs, means, and resources to enjoy their lives—that includes you too! As you look at the big picture of what you want to plant and, ultimately, harvest, keep in mind that it's not about "me," it's about the greater "we." What benefits all will benefit you, because we're all interconnected.

You must be very clear that *you are not your job.* The position you have, the grand title or the salary you receive, are not who you are. They are merely signs of "visible power." They don't define you. When you identify with your higher self, you're not reliant on statistics, bottom lines, or the economy to tell you whether you're valuable or to "complete" you in any way. You will embrace your true value and esteem. Understanding your divine nature is the key to unlocking everything you would like in your life. Because when you do, you operate in a creative, collaborative way that will affect the bottom line.

You and Your Team

The way to achieve power and influence is to empower others. To do so, you have to be able to trust. Otherwise, you'll try to control someone's every movement and the end result will reflect your fear and distrust. Allowing another person to blossom and grow will allow you to grow as well. However, you're the one to begin this cycle of growth. Empowering other people does not mean you're abdicating your own power. You are showing them that you yourself are growing and there is more than enough room for everyone to grow and share in the success.

However, there will be times when you will have unhappy staffers. This is probably the biggest hurdle any manager will ever face. It's important to recognize you are *not* responsible for their happiness. You are there to direct, encourage, and gently correct your team's course as you go. You're there to give your players the opportunities and resources they need to succeed and progress. Work to the best of your abilities, but remember the actions they take and the results are up to them. You cannot control them. They, not you, are responsible for their own personal happiness. It is essential that they make the choices that are best for them to achieve that happiness within themselves.

I have had staffers vehemently express their unhappiness to me. No matter what resources or opportunities I provided, they weren't happy. One even said, "Don't you care?! You're supposed to keep us happy, you know!" I simply looked at him and said, "No, you are responsible for your own happiness. Whether to be happy or not is your choice in life. My job is to provide you with all the resources and opportunities to succeed to the best of my ability. How you choose to use them is up to you."

When the people around you are resistant, keep in mind that they are who they need to be right here and right now. They have their lessons to learn and so do you. What is it that you need to learn? Irritating people are your greatest teachers. When they're grating on your nerves, look deep within yourself and ask, "Why is this behavior bothering me so much?" You may discover you need to strengthen a certain skill or correct some beliefs that are in sync with your ego self rather than your core values. If someone you're working with is causing you to feel frustrated or annoyed, be grateful. Without people like this, you wouldn't see what you have to correct in your own life. The powerful law of reflection causes you to interact with people who mirror the unaddressed issues inside of you.

- What is being mirrored back to you today?
- What lesson can you learn from that mirroring?

Forget Trying to Be Perfect

Perfection is a concept created by the ego self. The ego will whisper in your ear that you're not doing enough, you're not good enough, and you'll never "get it right." Perfection is the perception that to have the desired effect, you must be flawless and everything you do must be absolutely perfect. Perfection is the result of fear and insecurity bubbling to the surface. It's that "seek but do not find" line of thinking. Thank your ego self for sharing, then tell it to hit the road! My most influential mentor gave me a sage piece of advice: Just put one foot in front of the other and allow the universe to correct your course as you go. If you can remain open, listen, admit mistakes, and be aware of any adjustments you need to make, everything will be fine. However, if you don't start walking you'll never really know whether you can help others. So get out there!

Parting Words

This journey you're about to take is a spiritual journey. It is taken within the self and reflected in how you do business. As you move closer into operating from your highest potential, the transformation will roll out very subtly. It may take time and practice. You will find yourself at times repeating some of your old habits. Don't be discouraged. Give yourself the gifts of patience and compassion. Once you gain a deeper understanding that these old habitual reactions are no longer necessary or helpful, you will be able to let go of them and the shift inside of you will happen quickly.

Then you'll experience that magical moment when you're in the middle of your normal everyday activities and you now take an action or hear yourself saying words that come from your highest self without any effort. You'll be startled. But then you'll realize the real you is surfacing after a long suppression. The transformation in you will cause an alignment on the outside, and your business will transform in response.

Be a change agent, and be open to all that will change.

Acknowledgements

There are many people I wish to thank for contributing their special skills and talents to this project. First of all I would like to thank my friend and publishing consultant, Stephanie Gunning, for this book might never have been published without her help. Had it not been for her gentle, yet persistent, guidance in developing the manuscript and helping me see its potential, I would have been lost in my own head and might never have brought this book into being. I am grateful for the beautiful book cover design by the brilliant Kenneth Jansson. Special thanks also go to my editorial team, and to Lynn Serafinn who created the inside layout and my promotional campaign. I am also thankful for both my amazing assistants, Jamie Seitz and Lisa Jacobsen, who masterfully handled (and continue to handle) organizing, balancing, and keeping everything up to speed.

My sincere thanks also go to my friends Liz Pabon, Lisa Crisalle and Nancy Hipple for their constant support throughout this entire process. I am especially grateful to John Leonetti, who helped me find my truth and made sure I stayed on track. Without the love and support of my family, especially my brother Joe, I probably would have shelved this project forever. And of course I am eternally grateful for my loving partner, Valen Fleming, who provided a safe place for me to process my fears, and to learn to believe in myself on a deeper level so I could make the publishing of this book a reality.

Throughout my life I have been blessed with some truly awe-inspiring mentors and teachers. None have been as graceful or dignified as my dear friend Donna Giuliano, who taught me what it means to be a compassionate leader. And none have inspired me more than Bob Weiser, who showed me that being a powerful leader means to have the ability to bring people together and help them believe anything is possible. Both of you completely altered my perception of business and relationships, and for this I am forever grateful.

Special thanks to Les Brown, who shook me until I woke up! You would not let me leave your presence until I said I would do what I intended to do.

To Martha Hamilton Snyder, my spiritual teacher for many years, who held my hand and helped me to understand, you have been a gift in my life and an inspiration to my soul.

Enormous appreciation and thanks must go to Berny Dohrmann and the CEO Space family of outstanding entrepreneurs, business leaders, and mentors who have supported, encouraged, and endorsed this project every step of the way.

I am particularly grateful for the words of Caroline Myss, Dr. Deepak Chopra, Ernest D. Chu, Greg Reid, Thomas Troward, James Allen, Raymond Holliwell, David Richo, Shelly Lefkoe, Patricia Aburdene, Jack Canfield, John Hope Bryant, Bob Burg and especially

Marianne Williamson. Each has been a wonderful teacher and mentor through their works and, in some cases, personal conversations we've had along the way.

I gratefully acknowledge all my students over the years who taught me so much about life, love, business, and "engagement." At times it has been a painful journey, but in the end, every situation presented to me helped me to grow and learn more about myself.

I thank the many business associates, colleagues, and team members from whom I have had the great pleasure to learn.

I thank God for the opportunity to have experienced so many cultures, people, beliefs, and exchanges at all levels. Without these many players on the stage of life, I would not be able to see the things I see now, know what I know now, and be who I truly am.

Looking back, it is amazing to me to see just how many cheerleaders, teachers, wise sages, and friends I have had along the way! It just goes to show "the decision to accept" truly is "the decision to receive."

Appendix 1
Reading Group Guidelines

Discussing Healing the Corporate World: How Value-based Leadership Transforms Business from the Inside Out will help you bridge your learning into taking action on the principles shared in this book. Use the questions below to start a meaningful dialogue and build your understanding of how these concepts apply to your daily activities, interactions and engagements. I would encourage you to use these tools in both your personal and professional lives.

1) What has led you to feel powerless in the workplace and/or your business?

2) When you reflect on the concept of your thoughts creating your reality, do you see a connection to many of the events going on around you?

3) What negative aspects of others personalities irate and annoy you?

4) What inside of you is being reflected back to you in these annoyances that you need to remedy within yourself?

5) How has this shown up in your life?

6) What kind of Divine Chaos has occurred in your business, career or personal life recently?

7) What are 5 things you need to let go of but you are clinging onto for dear life? These are things that no longer serve you.

8) What revolutionary idea do you have that is not being heard? Why not?

9) Pause. Look closely around you. Where is the opportunity for this to be considered available to you right now?

10) In which season are you currently sitting?

11) In which season are the people on your staff currently sitting?

12) What are 3 actions you can take to antidote the situation?

13) What are your 3 most important values and why?

14) Where have you noticed a mindset of lack in your thinking?

15) What is the fear associated with that perception of lack?

16) Which aspects of the FARCE Syndrome are you acting out today?

17) Which aspects of the LAFF Method have you not deployed? Why?

18) Explain the difference between being a go-giver as opposed to a go-getter.

19) Which characteristics from the Change Agent Manifesto most resonate with you and why?

20) Which aspects of the four functions of a leader most resonate with you and why?

21) Where have you compromised another team member's self esteem? What was the motivation behind it?

22) What is the value make up of your team?

23) What deters you and your team from collaborating with others?

24) What can you do to plan for innovation and creativity in your role?

25) What are your biggest fears about using the principles in this book?

26) What is the biggest thrill for you in becoming a change agent?

27) Ultimately, what is it you want to change or impact in the world around you?

28) Why is this important to you?

29) Would you share this book with a friend or colleague? If so, why?

30) What is your action plan after reading this book? Start with 3 simple concepts then build on those going forward.

Appendix 2
Recommended Resources

I have been honored and blessed to have learned from some of the best minds, experts, and compassionate teachers the world has to offer. Sometimes their wisdom was imparted to me personally. Other times illuminated to me by their words in book form. I am a voracious reader and I encourage you too to devour all you can on the topics of mental science, spirituality, and the power of leadership. I am sure these resources will enrich your journey as they have mine.

Awakening the Mind, Lightening the Heart. His Holiness the Dalai Lama. San Francisco, CA: Harper San Francisco, 1995.

Blue Ocean Strategy: How to Create Uncontested Market Space and Make the Competition Irrelevant. W. Chan Kim and Renée Mauborgne. Boston, MA: Harvard Business Press, 2005.

Common Purpose: How Great Leaders Get Organizations to Achieve the Extraordinary. Joel Kurtzman. New York: Jossey-Bass/Wiley, 2010.

Emotional Intelligence 2.0. Travis Bradberry and Jean Greaves. San Diego, CA: TalentSmart, 2009.

The Edinburgh and Dore Lectures on Mental Science. Thomas Troward. Radford, VA: Wilder Publications, 2007.

The Four Agreements. Don Miguel Ruiz. San Rafael, California: Amber-Allen Publishing, 1997.

The Go-Giver: A Little Story About a Powerful Business Idea. Bob Burg and John David Mann. New York: Portfolio by Penguin Group, 2007.

Invisible Acts of Power: Channeling Grace in Your Everyday Life. Caroline Myss. New York: Free Press, 2004.

Love Leadership: The New Way to Lead in a Fear-Based World. John Hope Bryant. New York: Jossey-Bass/Wiley, 2009.

Open Your Mind to Receive. Catherine Ponder. Camarillo, CA: DeVorss Publications, 1983. Revised 2003.

The Power of Kindness: The Unexpected Benefits of Leading a Compassionate Life. Piero Ferrucci. New York: Jeremy P. Tarcher/Penguin, 2006.

The Power of Your Supermind: Great Cosmic Wisdom Explained in a Clear and Practical Way. Vernon Howard. Pine, Arizona: New Life Foundation, 1975. Reprinted 2001.

Quantum Shift in the Global Brain: How the New Scientific Reality Can Change Us and Our World. Ervin Laszlo. Rochester, Vermont: Inner Traditions, 2008.

Riding the Waves of Innovation: Harness the Power of Global Culture to Drive Creativity and Growth. Fons Trompenaars and Charles Hampden-Turner. New York: McGraw Hill, 2010.

The Seven Spiritual Laws of Success: A Practical Guide to the Fulfillment of Your Dreams. Deepak Chopra. San Rafael, California: Amber-Allen Publishing, 1997.

Shadow Dance: Liberating the Power & Creativity of Your Dark Side. David Richo. Boston, MA: Shambhala Publications, Inc., 1999

The Success Principles: How to Get From Where You Are to Where You Want to Be. Jack Canfield. New York: Harper Collins, 2005.

Think & Grow Rich! Napoleon Hill. New York: Fawcett Books, 1960.

Working With The Law. Raymond Holiwell. BN Publishing, 2007.

You2: A High-Velocity Formula for Multiplying Your Personal Effectiveness in Quantum Leaps. Price Pritchett.

Your Invisible Power. Genevieve Behrend. Rockville, Maryland: Arc Manor, 2007.

Maria Gamb

As a former Fortune 500 trailblazer, Maria Gamb served for twenty-plus years as an executive in businesses valued at upwards of 100 million dollars. What were her keys to corporate success? Her ability to blend creativity, divine inspiration, and straightforward communication. Now, as the founder, CEO, and "Chief Change Agent" of NMS Communications, she shares her vast business skills, life experience, and knowledge of universal laws to help executives and entrepreneurs alike claim their ability to lead profitable, effective businesses that provide great value to those they serve.

Ms. Gamb believes a new breed of leadership is emerging, which bridges the gap between the harsh practicalities of business and the intuitive nature of Spirit—and it's this gap that she bridges with her own lecturing and teaching.

Ms. Gamb's career has taken her across the globe. She has lived for significant periods in Australia and England, and worked in countless others. Her understanding and appreciation of cultural differences and the inner workings of different kinds of industries and their leadership make her a force to be reckoned with in the global business landscape.

Ms. Gamb works from a loft in Brooklyn, New York, where she pursues her passion to help businesspeople transform the world through her one-on-one and group executive mentoring programs, sales of online products, and public speaking.

❖ Learn More ❖

Maria Gamb offers a variety of learning and teaching opportunities through her websites:

www.HealingTheCorporateWorld.com
www.MariaGamb.com

We invite you to join the *Change Agent* weekly ezine for more tools and tips to walking into your exceptional leadership role in this world. This publication is free of charge and is our way of supporting the growing number of Change Agents to stay informed and inspired on their journey. To get your free subscription, visit www.MariaGamb.com

Seminars and Workshops

Maria provides national and international workshops, seminars and keynote speeches on the topics of leadership, corporate self-esteem, transformation, navigating change as well as innovation and creativity. For smaller groups of entrepreneurs and executives she offers the Change Agent Academy™ learning modules and retreats several times during the year. As well as the customized dynamic creativity think tank process for transforming business platforms, strategies and product development called Thinkubation™.

Private Coaching & Mentoring

Maria accepts a handful of talented, driven entrepreneurs and business leaders who want to refine their leadership skills and forge a new path where they currently are working or in creating a new business for the future. This program is for serious thought leaders, pioneers, heretics and change agents who sincerely want to make a difference in the world by walking into their highest potential.

Corporate Events

Through a variety of private workshops and retreats Maria works with corporate teams to unlock the organizations change agents special skills, power and influence that bolsters the bottom line...and have fun doing it too!

To find out more about these programs go to
www.MariaGamb.com/services.html

NMS Communications LLC
900 3rd Avenue P.O. Box 320611
Brooklyn, NY 11232
Phone: (800) 527-8186
Email: info@mariagamb.com